4-4-2

A SOURCE BOOK

EDITED AND ANNOTATED BY

Dennis Casteele

Bookman Publishing/Baltimore, Maryland

Printed in the U.S.A.
Copyright 1983 in U.S.A. by Bookman Dan!, Inc.

ISBN 0-934780-12-9

First Edition
Fifth Printing

Inquiries may be directed to:
Bookman Dan!, Inc.
P.O. Box 13492
Baltimore, Maryland 21203

Contents

Preface

The 4-4-2s were really the second generation of high performance transportation to come from Oldsmobile. Introduced in late 1964, after rival GM division Pontiac had gotten out of the gate with its phenominally successful GTO lineup, the 4-4-2s gradually became one of the best handling, fastest and most appealing automotive groups ever offered in the domestic market.

Oldsmobile is built on one of the most solid foundations in automotive history. Its origins can be traced directly to 1897 when automotive pioneer R. E. Olds and a group of associates built a handful of rather primitive gasoline-powered motor carriages. By 1901, Olds had dialed in the right combination and his agile, little Curved Dash Oldsmobiles were the darlings of the motoring public. For a while, Oldsmobile's only problem was building its cars fast enough and here Olds was an assembly line pioneer when Henry Ford was only dreaming about mass production. Oldsmobile continued to offer the Curved Dash runabout through 1907, but, by 1904, the company opted to build larger, more powerful, and vastly more expensive, cars. This caused R. E. Olds to leave his namesake company in 1904. He immediately found new and even stronger financial backing and, by 1905, he was setting up a huge auto manufacturing complex—the REO Motor Car Company—a few blocks from Oldsmobile's Lansing plant. By 1908, Oldsmobile had slipped rather badly in the marketplace, but wheeling and dealing Billy Durant used the Olds nameplate as a cornerstone in founding General Motors. For the next few decades, Oldsmobile set about offering steady and solid transportation that fit nicely into the GM master plan. Gradually, Olds acquired the tag as the "GM innovator." The first innovations came with various nickel, and then chrome, plating techniques. Olds was also a leader in the volume production of closed cars and pioneered various new painting procedures. The first Olds blockbuster, however, came on the 1940 models with the introduction of the automatic HydraMatic transmission. While certainly not the first automatic gearbox (Olds offered a "semi-automatic" as early as 1937 and crosstown rival Reo had its "Self-Shifter" much earlier), the HydraMatic was the best unit to that date.

After World War II, Olds entered its first performance era with the high-winding V-8 known as the Rocket. Until the small block Chevies and monster Hemis came into fashion, the Rocket 88 was King of the Highways. From 1949 until 1957, the Futuramic Oldsmobiles offered good performance levels, particularly the 88 series. The era was capped in 1957 with the tri-carb J-2 performance package, but, by then, the rest of the industry had caught—and even passed—Olds with the aforementioned Chrysler and Chevy V-8s, fuel injection packages from Chevrolet and Pontiac and even factory supercharging from Ford.

With the "chrome-mobiles" offered by the auto industry in general in 1958—and General Motors' divisions, in particular—Olds went in a new direction. The J-2 lasted into the 1958 model year and Lee Petty managed a Daytona 500 victory in a 1959 Olds, but performance was a lame duck at Olds for a few years.

Whatever the General Motors game plan was, Oldsmobile had a prominent role to play. In the very early 1960s, a group of compacts was introduced by GM. First came the radical Corvairs from Chevy in 1960, followed by the Buick Special, Pontiac Tempest and Olds F-85. The little Olds was sharp unit with a nifty aluminum-block, 215 cid V-8 underhood. A glimmer of performance was managed in 1962 and 1963 as Olds offered a limited edition F-85 coupe known as the Jetfire. This car was boosted by a turbocharged V-8 underhood and some sporty external trimmings, but at best it was a limited marketing success.

A bright Spring day in 1965 found me venturing into an Olds dealership in Tipp City, Ohio, on a car shopping mission. What I had in mind was a couple-of-year-old used car. Rather quickly—and I might add with very little arm twisting—a salesman had me behind the wheel of a Target Red 1965 F-85 club coupe with the 4-4-2 performance package. I've driven a number of hot cars as a journalistic automotive road tester, member of a car company PR staff, and even as a professional auto racer. That 4-4-2 still stands out in my mind as one of the best balanced performance cars I've ever had the pleasure of driving. I was hooked then and there, but the financial realities set in, finally, and I settled for a used 1957 Corvette which cost me about a grand less than the 4-4-2.

Oldsmobile has always been rather hung-up on numbering some of its cars rather than naming them. In the early going, the Curved Dash runabout was officially known as the 6-C. Subsequently came the Model 23s, Model 47s, Model 45s and so on. By 1939, Olds offered several series of cars including a 60, 70 and 90 series. The complete model designation was determined by adding the number of engine cylinders to the series designation. There were 66s and 68s, 76s and 78s and 98s and, for a couple of years, even a 96. By 1949, the potent 88 series was born by crossing a lightweight 76 body with the all-new Rocket V-8 powerplant from a 98. Today, the Ninety-Eight and Eighty-Eight nameplates survive—even though the logic behind the system has long since disappeared. It seemed logical, then, that Oldsmobile would use numbers to tag its performance cars rather than the catchy names like "GTO," "Gran Sport" and "Super Sport" used by other GM divisions. Upon introduction in 1964, the 4-4-2 designation stood for four-speed transmission, four-barrel carburetion and two (dual) exhausts. In 1965, this was amended to have the first "4" stand for 400 cid, rather than four-speed transmission. Thereafter, things changed but the nameplate stayed the same. There were 4-4-2s that had more than 400 cid, more than four-barrels of carburetion and even some later models with less than dual exhausts—but the nameplate was fixed and it hung on until the end of the line in 1980.

While Oldsmobile did not have a headline grabbing management "face" like "Bunky" Knudsen or John DeLorean in its ranks, it did have one of the most talented auto executives to ever draw a General Motors paycheck in John B. Beltz. An engineer by trade, and a genuine car enthusiast to boot, Beltz was responsible for much of the thinking that went into the creation and improvement of the 4-4-2 and Toronado programs. During the late 1960s and early 1970s, I was working as a member of the automotive press and, let me tell you, John Beltz was a writer's dream come true. Here was a guy who knew cars inside and out and absolutely loved to talk about them. I remember one afternoon conversation with him that covered everything from Curved Dash Oldsmobiles to Ferraris. By 1969, Beltz had gone the traditional Olds management route from chief engineer to general manager. He most certainly was on a rather rapid path which would have led to the GM hierarchy as either president or board chairman. In 1972, I joined the Oldsmobile public relations staff and my lone regret was that earlier that year John Beltz had died.

Beltz was by no means the only talent in Olds management or the only one who knew performance. The current Olds chief engineer, Bob Dorshimer, is a great engineer and is very knowledgeable on performance autos. Dale Smith, now retired from the Oldsmobile engineering department, for years was the Olds racing and performance connection. "General Dale" was a fixture for many years in the pit areas at major drag races and oval track stock car events. In summary, it was Beltz, and to a lesser degree fellows like Dorshimer and Smith, who made the 4-4-2s the solid performers they were.

While performance oriented models like the GTO, Z-28 Camaro and various hot Mustangs entered the world with a lot of fanfare, the Olds 4-4-2 kind of sneaked up on all of us. In the early planning stages for this book, publisher Tom Bonsall and I were pretty well in accord on the path it should take. Then, Tom said, "Of course, we want to lead this thing off as strongly as we can with as much 1964 4-4-2 stuff as possible." I grinned at that since Tom was drawing on a lot of his own Pontiac background. That GM division introduced both the GTO and Firebird with great hoopla. Olds almost sneaked out its first 4-4-2s! There was a single (and quite rare) dealer sheet on the car and a lone factory photo. That was just about it!! By 1965, the marketing and promotional folks caught up with the engineers and built a solid communication program to tell performance enthusiasts about the 4-4-2.

Tom and I have carefully plotted the scope of this volume. It covers the run of the 4-4-2s, 1964-1980. Also worthy of serious attention are the Hurst/Olds models, the mighty W-cars and the lone year (1970) Rallye 350s. I enthusiastically support the overall format of Bookman's source books and, as a long-time literature collector, I appreciate the concept. In fact, it was in the early 1970s that I met Tom Bonsall at an automotive swap meet in Columbus, Ohio. I usually saw Tom at Carlisle, Spring and Fall, and watched with no small interest his rise in automotive publishing circles. I appreciate his marketing efforts at Bookman Dan and their enthusiastic marketing of my Crestline book, "The Cars of Oldsmobile."

Despite a decade of friendship and parallel interests in serious literature collecting and writing, it took a mutual friend—Ohio literature baron, Sam Shields—to suggest we get together on a volume such as this one. From that point on, things progressed rapidly and fell into place very well.

There is no doubt the Cutlass/F-85 based performance cars from Olds—particularly those from 1964-1972—are quite collectible. Mike Fusick, a veteran in the parts vending business, notes that all indications are these cars are headed toward popularity levels previously achieved by 1955-57 Chevies and the early Mustangs. These collectible 4-4-2s offered a balance of straight line performance, handling and super appearance, and offered it for a relatively small amount of money. In fact, the 1964 4-4-2 option package was largely put together from the list of items offered to police departments in various packages. For those desiring more performance yet, there were the awesome "W-cars," some of which carried warnings in factory literature that they were not intended for street use. While not of the performace level of an all-out W-car, the rare Hurst/Oldsmobiles offered a nice blend of luxury, good looks and more than adequate performance.

From 1964 through 1967, the 4-4-2 was an optional package on various F-85 and Cutlass models. From 1968 through 1971, the 4-4-2 stood as a separate model within the F-85/Cutlass group. In 1972, various safety and pollution regulations hit the domestic car builders hard and performance, at least at the factory level, was a dead issue. At this point, the 4-4-2 was returned to optional status. In subsequent years, the package centered mainly on equipment that made 4-4-2s handle a bit better and look racier than standard Cutlass offering.

Some extremely rare and informative sales literature and photos are shared with you in this volume. In a few years, Olds offered specific literature on the 4-4-2 and its other intermediate performance cars. Most other years saw the performace machinery well covered in the main catalogue. In some cases, rare information, usually designed for dealership employees only and printed in extremely small quanties, has been reprinted in this source book. Some specific literature exists on the Hurst/Olds, W-machines and Rallye 350 and much of that material is contained herein. Factory photos, including our color cover shot, are used to further communicate information on the 4-4-2s and companion performance cars.

I would be remiss if I did not offer thanks to several people for helping me assemble this book. First and foremost I would like to thank Tom Bonsall and Bookman Publishing for their entire Source Book series and the chance to include Oldsmobile in the group. Oldsmobile Division's public relations department, under the directorship of F. W. Bennetts, has been helpful in researching this book. I've done a great deal of writing on a variety of Oldsmobile topics over the years—books, magazines, newsletters and newspaper articles—and Helen Earley of Olds PR is always the first person I turn to for help. This volume was no exception and, again, Mrs. Earley provided us with a wealth of information.

Hopefully, this source book will be the first of several published on Oldsmobile. In the future, we would like to cover other Cutlass models, the front-drive Toronados and perhaps the mighty Rockets from 1949-1957.

Thank you for your interest in the 4-4-2 based performance Oldsmobiles. We sincerely hope you enjoy this source book.

Lansing, Michigan
January, 1982

1964

Sales of 546,112 units netted Oldsmobile a sixth place standing in the industry sales race in 1964. Most of the production run was still devoted to traditional American full-size cars, but the new, smaller cars were starting to generate serious attention.

By 1964, the F-85/Cutlass series had, indeed, matured to the point where it was becoming an important part of the Olds model mix. The F-85 had come a long way since the little aluminum-engined unit first hit the auto scene in 1961. Looming large in the immediate F-85/Cutlass future was the performance image and the creation of the 4-4-2 package.

Cross-state rival, Pontiac, introduced its GTO with the publicity guns blazing, but Olds almost sneaked up on the motoring public with its 4-4-2 machines. The 4-4-2 was a mid-year introduction and was Oldsmobile's first all-out performance job since the J-2 cars of 1957 and 1958. In the 1962 and 1963 model years, Olds had had a slight flirtation with performance with the turbocharged Jetfire Cutlass coupes.

Actually, little new was created for the 4-4-2. Instead, long-standing equipment was grabbed off the shelf, including the police pursuit packages Olds had offered for years. The 4-4-2 designation in the first year stood for four-barrel carburetion, four-speed transmission on the floor and two (dual) exhausts. The package was option B-09 and it was available on any F-85 V-8 model except the station wagon. This package consisted of special items like heavy-duty shocks, springs, and new rear stabilizer bar, dual-snorkel air cleaner and premium quality rod and main bearings. The underhood heart of the 4-4-2 was a 330 cid, 310 hp Rocket V-8. This was a premium-fueled engine and a really decent performer. Although the 1964 4-4-2 was a well kept secret from most of the car buying public—only 2,999 of them were bought that year—it was a tough street performer that offered as much balanced performance as could be obtained from any showroom stocker of the era.

Factory literature is close to non-existent for this introductory year. Number 8 in a series of product selling information bulletins—issued by Oldsmobile's merchandising department—is probably the most complete data issued. It carried the title, "A Hot New Number...Olds 4-4-2." It is a two-color sheet printed on both sides and punched for a dealer data booklet or three-ring binder (see pages 9-10). The factory issued at least one press release on a 4-4-2 outfitted Cutlass

The large Olds color catalogue for 1964 devotes six pages to F-85 and Cutlass models, but it was layed out and printed months before the 4-4-2 package was finalized and offered to the public. Olds began issuing a misnamed "sports car" catalogue in 1963 and the 1964 color version of that catalogue again was issued long before the 4-4-2 concept was finalized. The sports car piece gave two pages to the Olds intermediates. Other machinery featured included the Starfire and the ill-fated Jetstar. All in all, anything in print on the 1964 4-4-2 is very rare, although there was some nice coverage for the other F-85's and Cutlasses.

1964 Oldsmobile

PRODUCT SELLING INFORMATION

No. 8

A Hot New Number...

OLDS 442

Police Needed It – Olds Built It – Pursuit Proved It

New "4-4-2" Features Deliver Superb Performance!

-BARREL CARBURETION plus high-lift cams boost power of the "4-4-2" Ultra High-Compression V-8 to 310 h.p. — up 20 h.p. over Cutlass V-8.

-ON-THE-FLOOR stick shift synchromesh transmission captures every power advantage both up and down the entire gear range.

DUAL EXHAUSTS—complete dual exhaust system features less back pressure for better performance . . . aluminized for longer life.

PLUS:

- Heavy-duty shocks and springs provide smoother cornering . . . better pitch control.

- New rear stabilizer bar reduces roll, provides flatter cornering, better handling.

- Dual snorkel air cleaner improves engine breathing.

- Higher lift camshaft helps boost power performance.

- Extra-high-quality rod and main bearings mean longer life in high-performance driving.

NOTE: Order under Option #B09 . . . Available in any F-85 V-8 model except station wagon.

Sensational New Power Team Gives "4-4-2" That Extra Performance!

The "4-4-2", with a 4-speed synchromesh transmission, has a 330-cu.-in. V-8 engine designed to deliver more power than ever before. At 5200 rpm, it develops 310 h.p. . . *20 h.p. more than a standard Cutlass V-8!* And there is 355 lb.-ft. of torque at 3600 rpm. Owners get the kind of power from the "4-4-2" that can push its weight around easily!

The power team of the "4-4-2" is a proved performer! It has been used by law enforcement agencies who needed a car that could accelerate rapidly, pursue at high speeds and idle for long periods without stalling. That same power team is now available in any F-85 V-8 except station wagons.

Many new engineering improvements have been added throughout the entire car. A new camshaft gives higher valve lift and longer overlap. The dual snorkel air cleaner provides better engine breathing. New, heavy-duty aluminum crankshaft bearings mean longer life in a high-performance engine.

The excellent handling of the "4-4-2" matches its outstanding power performance. Heavy-duty springs are rated at 410 lb. in the front and 160 lb. in the rear. *This is an increase of 30% over the standard Cutlass V-8.* The front stabilizer bar is bigger for better control of lean

and roll on high-speed cornering . . . and the "4-4-2" is *one of the few* American cars to have a heavy-duty *rear* stabilizer bar . . . to improve performance handling characteristics.

Every way you look at it . . . "4-4-2" adds up to outstanding performance from a sensational performer!

New Low-Profile "Red-Line" Tires Are Standard on the "4-4-2"

This 7.50 x 14" Red-Line tire has a lower, wider contour to reduce flexing and heat build-up. It also has a tough nylon cord body for extra durability and safety. The red line on the tire is an action identification for the "4-4-2"!

Three Bright "4-4-2" Medallions . . . One On Each Front Fender And One On The Rear Deck . . . Let You Know That This Is Oldsmobile's Hot New Number!

OLDSMOBILE... WHERE THE ACTION IS!

OLDSMOBILE DIVISION, GENERAL MOTORS CORPORATION • LITHO IN U.S.A.

This model year saw the marketing types catch up with the engineers, and Olds let the world know about the 4-4-2. Overall, Olds held onto sixth place in the sales standings with 591,701 total sales. The intermediate F-85/Cutlass group continued to be an important part of the Olds sales mix.

In 1965, the 4-4-2 option could be ordered on the F-85 club coupe, Cutlass sport coupe, Cutlass holiday coupe or Cutlass convertible. A new engine package was centered on a 400 cid Rocket V-8 which turned out 345 hp, up 30 hp from the 1964 4-4-2 package. The engine utilized its own special cylinder block casting, pistons, exhaust manifolds and heavy-duty cooling system. Transmission selection ranged from either a column-shifted or console-controlled, heavy-duty Jetaway automatic to a heavy-duty, three-speed manual unit or a floor-shifted, fully-synchronized, close-ratio four-speed.

The 4-4-2 continued to be a balanced machine and it was excellent in the handling department. Heavy-duty components there included: bigger springs, shock absorbers and hefty front and rear stabilizer bars. Larger 7.75x14 inch redline nylon tires were mounted on heavy-duty, six inch rims.

External 4-4-2 emblems up front, at the rear and on the sculptured side panels gave the special package instant identification on the street. The 4-4-2 also enjoyed a special grille treatment in 1965. In the F-85 version, the 4-4-2 package cost $190.45, with a list price of $156.02 for Cutlass models fitted with it. For this year, a number of options could be ordered to personalize a Cutlass or F-85. These included: four-season air conditioning, anti-spin rear axle, sports console, custom steering wheel, tilt steering wheel and wire wheel discs.

Publicity and literature on the 4-4-2 became much more abundant in 1965. "Hot Rod" magazine's Eric Rickman tested the F-85 coupe version of the 4-4-2. He concluded, "Emphatically, the 4-4-2 remained one of the most likable machines we have ever had the pleasure to drive. At the going price of $2,799, this Olds is really a buyer's bargain; we wish there were more of them." A total of 25,003 buyers apparently agreed with his assessment (3,468 of whom picked the convertible).

The first literature exclusive to the 4-4-2 made its appearance in 1965. It was an unimpressive little folder with no color in it, but it was all 4-4-2—and it came in two editions, the later, revised version of which is illustrated here (see pages 12-13).* The 4-4-2 package shared a two-page spread in the various 1965 full-line color catalogues with the other F-85 and Cutlass offerings (see page 14).* Olds printed a special color catalogue on its 1965 "sports" models. Sharing this catalogue were the Starfire, Jetstar I and F-85 V-6 sports coupe. Clearly, the 4-4-2 was the feature car of the group as it rated a two-page center section entitled, "Winning combination to an exciting new world of action" (see pages 16-17).* Lastly, a full-line engines catalogue included a full-page spread on the 4-4-2 (see page 15).* The motoring press was also treated to a special press kit liberally quoting Olds general manager, Harold Metzel, a complete specification sheet, a pair of glossy factory photos and a copy of the 1965 full-line color catalogue—all packaged in a special 4-4-2 cover.

*Front covers shown below.

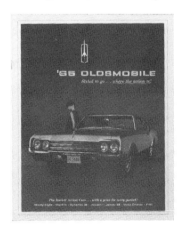

THE "INSIDE TRACK" ON OLDS' HOTTEST NUMBER . . .

STANDARD FEATURES ON ALL 4-4-2s

- Heavy-Duty Guard-Beam Frame
- Heavy-Duty Front and Rear Shock Absorbers
- Heavy-Duty Front and Rear Springs
- Heavy-Duty Radiator
- Heavy-Duty Propeller Shaft
- Heavy-Duty Front Engine Mountings
- Heavy-Duty Clutch with Synchromesh
- Heavy-Duty Battery
- Oversize Dual Exhaust
- Heavy-Duty Front and Rear Stabilizer Bar
- Heavy-Duty Wheels
- 7.75 x 14" Red-Line Nylon Tires
- Special 4-4-2 Grille, Emblems
- Smaller Rear Fender Scoops

AVAILABLE FACTORY-INSTALLED AXLE RATIOS

With 3- or 4-Speed Manual Transmission	With Jetaway Transmission
3.55 to 1	3.23 to 1
3.90 to 1	3.55 to 1
	3.90 to 1

OTHER AVAILABLE AXLE RATIOS (Dealer-Installed Package)

4.11 to 1	4.33 to 1

1. All ratios available with anti-spin differential.
2. If a 4.11 or 4.33 ratio is to be dealer installed, the buyer should order a 3.55 or 3.90 axle from the factory.

4-4-2 AVAILABLE IN FOLLOWING BODY STYLES

	Shipping Weight (lbs.)	MSRP*
Club Coupe	3398	$2605
Sports Coupe	3450	2799
Holiday Coupe	3474	2940
Convertible	3576	3139

*Manufacturer's Suggested Retail Prices. Includes reimbursement for Federal Excise Tax and suggested dealer delivery and handling charge.

Some of the convenience and appearance features shown in this folder are available at modest extra cost. Information is available at your dealer's.

Oldsmobile reserves the right to make changes at any time, without notice in colors, materials, equipment and specifications and models, and to discontinue models.

OLDSMOBILE DIVISION • GENERAL MOTORS CORP. • LITHO IN U.S.A.

REVISED 11/65

The HORSEPOWER Story

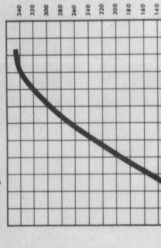

The TORQUE Story

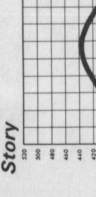

CHECK THESE SPECS
against the world's leading high-performance sports cars

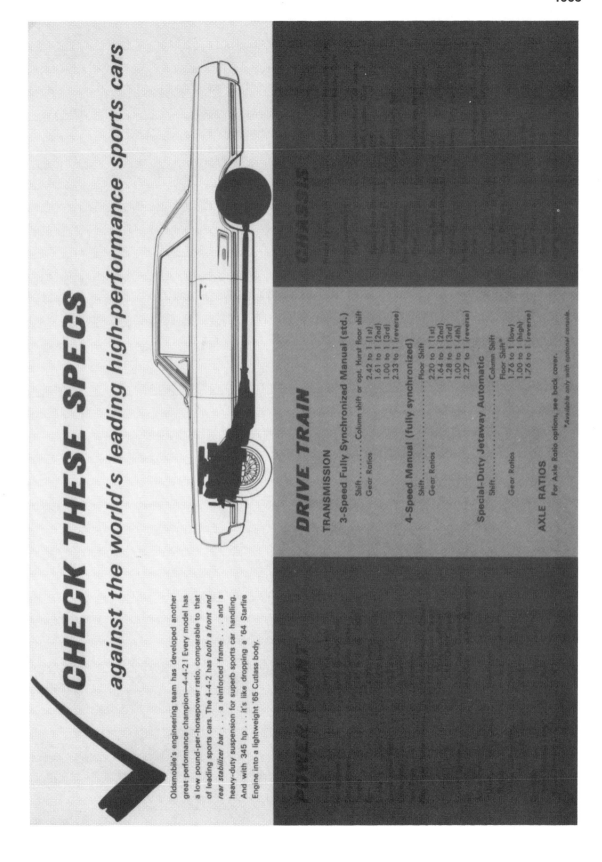

Oldsmobile's engineering team has developed another great performance champion—4-4-2! Every model has a low pound-per-horsepower ratio, comparable to that of leading sports cars. The 4-4-2 has *both a front and rear stabilizer bar* . . . *a reinforced frame* . . . and *a heavy-duty suspension* for superb sports car handling. And with 345 hp . . . it's like dropping a '64 Starfire Engine into a lightweight '65 Cutlass body.

POWER PLANT

CHASSIS

DRIVE TRAIN

TRANSMISSION

3-Speed Fully Synchronized Manual (std.)

Shift	Column shift or opt. Hurst floor shift
Gear Ratios	2.42 to 1 (1st)
	1.61 to 1 (2nd)
	1.00 to 1 (3rd)
	2.33 to 1 (reverse)

4-Speed Manual (fully synchronized)

Shift	Floor Shift
Gear Ratios	2.20 to 1 (1st)
	1.64 to 1 (2nd)
	1.28 to 1 (3rd)
	1.00 to 1 (4th)
	2.27 to 1 (reverse)

Special-Duty Jetaway Automatic

Shift	Column Shift
	Floor Shift*
Gear Ratios	1.76 to 1 (low)
	1.00 to 1 (high)
	1.76 to 1 (reverse)

AXLE RATIOS

For Axle Ratio options, see back cover.

*Available only with optional console.

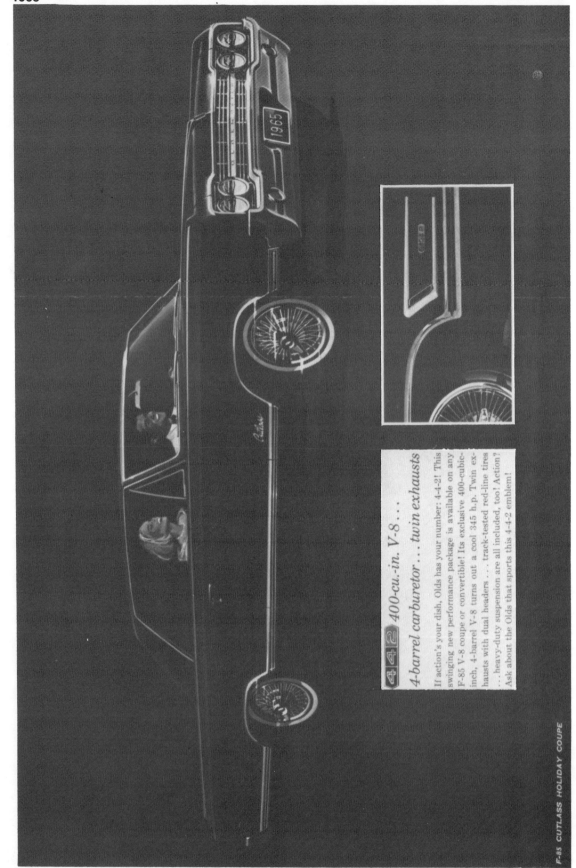

4-4-2 *400-cu.-in. V-8 . . . 4-barrel carburetor . . . twin exhausts*

If action's your dish, Olds has your number: 4-4-2! This swinging new performance package is available on any F-85 V-8 coupe or convertible! Its exclusive 400-cubic-inch, 4-barrel V-8 turns out a cool 345 h.p. Twin exhausts with dual headers . . . track-tested red-line tires . . . heavy-duty suspension are all included, too! Action? Ask about the Olds that sports this 4-4-2 emblem!

F-85 CUTLASS HOLIDAY COUPE

442 Hot New Number...
Great New Performance

4 400-Cubic-Inch Displacement
345-Horsepower Brand-New V-8

4 Four-Barrel Carburetion Plus
High-Lift Cam for More Power

2 Dual Exhausts Reduce Back
Pressure for Even Better
Performance

OLDSMOBILE 4-4-2 CONVERTIBLE

If "go" is what you're looking for, you've got the green light the instant you step into an Olds 4-4-2 with this great new performance package. Choose the car—the F-85 V-8 Club Coupe or the Cutlass Holiday Coupe, Sports Coupe or Convertible is made to move out with this 4-4-2 Performance Package. It's as easy as 1-2-3 to make the move to real action. Any of 3 transmissions lets you capture every power advantage. Aluminized dual exhausts last longer. Heavy-duty chassis performance package provides the kind of chassis required to make the most of this "hot" new number.

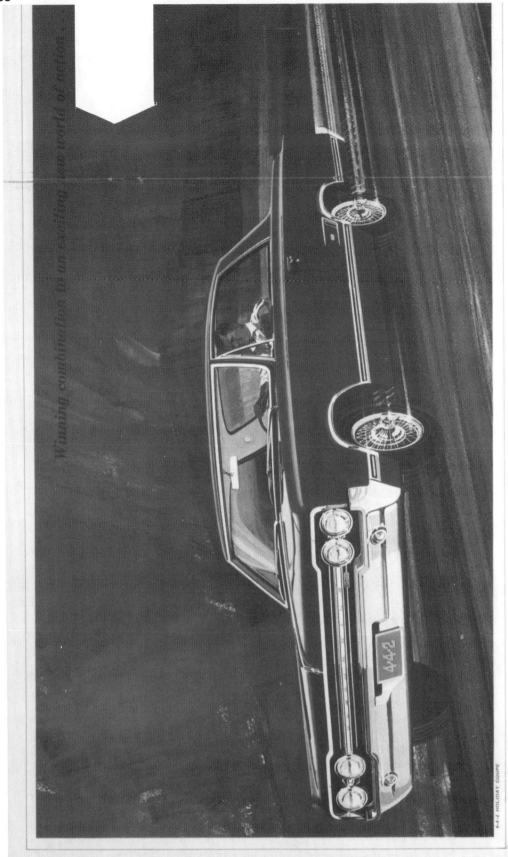

Winning combination in an exciting new world of action.

4-4-2 HOLIDAY COUPE

OLDSMOBILE 4-4-2

400-cubic-inch V-8, four-barrel carburetor, dual exhausts, track-tested redline tires, special heavy-duty chassis components—all in one Olds package!

No wonder it's a hot number! Just look at its arithmetic! 400 cubes of V-8 engine! 345 horses. 440 lb.-ft. of torque. 10.25-to-1 compression. Four-barrel carb. Twin pipes. And 3.55-to-1 rear-axle ratio. Add a heavy-duty suspension with high-rate springs and shocks. Heavy stabilizer bars, front and rear. A set of track-tested red-line shoes. Plus a three-speed synchromesh gear box. (Extra-cost options: Jetaway automatic, or four-on-the-floor for the purists!) Sum total: 4-4-2—just the number you've been waiting for! And it's yours on any F-85 V-8 coupe or convertible!

Four-barrel carb—standard!

Spirited 400-cubic-inch V-8!

Under that stylish rear end—twin aluminized exhaust pipes!

The 4-4-2 continued to gain strength in 1966—but most of the glory and headlines went to the revolutionary, front-wheel drive Toronado first introduced by Olds for this model year. Total sales of 594,069 vaulted the Lansing car builder into fourth place in industry sales.

Option status continued to be accorded the 4-4-2. The package, option L-78, cost $185.07 on an F-85 club coupe or F-85 holiday coupe. On a Cutlass, the 4-4-2 package cost $151.61 and it was offered on the sports coupe, holiday coupe or convertible. A total of 21,997 found buyers.

True high performance folks looked down the equipment list to option number L-69. It offered all the normal 4-4-2 engine, transmission and handling goodies. The big boom in the L-69 package, however, came from a three two-barrelled carburetion set-up—the first such factory offering since Olds dropped the J-2 package in 1958. The tri-carb 4-4-2 package was list-priced at $264.54 and it was a rarely seen accessory. This ultimate 4-4-2 offering put out 360 hp—an underrated 10 more than the standard four-barrelled 4-4-2 motor.

There were a host of special 4-4-2 features for 1966. Transmission selection could be made from three-speed manual units, either column- or Hurst floor-shifted, wide-ratio or close-ratio Hurst floor-shifted four-speed manuals or a special-duty Jetaway automatic. Rear end selection offered eight axle ratio choices, ranging from 3.23 to 1 to 4.33 to 1. Handling improvement items included: stiffer springs, stabilizer bars at both ends, wide rims and redline nylon cord tires. A deep rumbling sound came from the special, low-restriction exhaust system. Exhaust pipes were a full two inches in diameter, capped by special chrome extensions.

The option list for the Olds intermediate models continued to grow. It included: A-41, four-way power seat, $69; A-91, power trunk release, $12; C-08, vinyl roof covering, $83; D-55, sports console, $67; G-80, anti-spin rear axle, $41; J-50, power brakes, $41; N-40, power steering, $94; N-95, wire wheel discs, $69; V-16, tachometer, $52; and V-80, bi-phonic rear radio speaker, $15.

In its third year, product literature was abundant on the 4-4-2 package. The small version of the full-line color catalogue gave full-page treatment to the 4-4-2.* Olds continued its "sports models" catalogue in 1966 with a 16-page color edition, and the same basic art and text from the full-line catalogue was repeated, only more so (see pages 25-26).* More than half of that printed piece was devoted to the all-new Toronado. A first in 1966 was an exclusive 8x10, six-panel, color folder on just the 4-4-2. The headline on this piece was, "Looking for Action," and it probably was the most complete piece of literature Oldsmobile had produced to date on a performance car (see pages 19-24).* Relevant pages from the dealer data book are reproduced on pages 27-30.

*Front covers shown below.

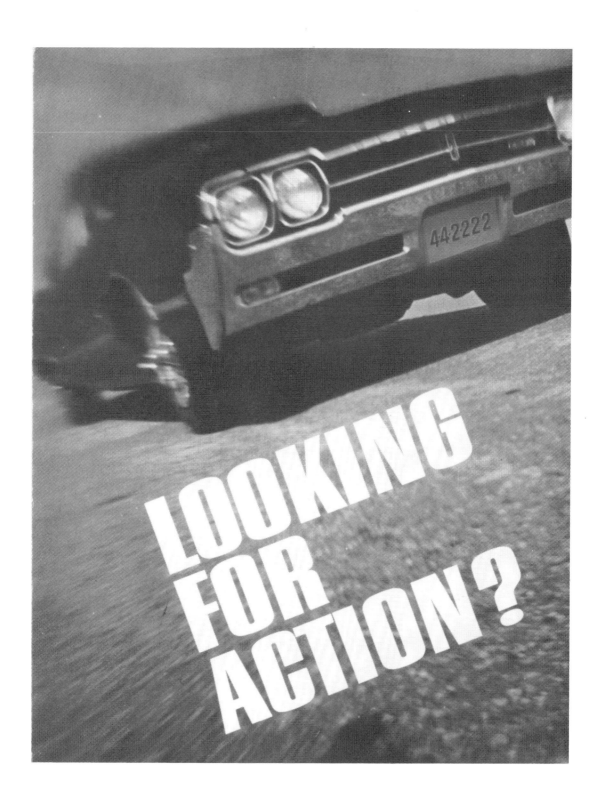

THERE IS MORE ACTION...

4-4-2 Performance V-8

The 400-cubic-inch block beats out balanced action with up to 360 horsepower. Rugged, the man wants to know? As a rock! Extra-large valves, specially designed intake manifold, Fire-Swirl combustion. Things like that. So turn it on. Tinker with it. Make it dance to your tune.

Quadrajet 4-Barrel Carburetor

Great, standard step-out feature for the 1966 4-4-2. Includes smaller primary bores, a more sensitive automatic choke! A hard-working team for cruising economy! And when you step out and cut in with the bigger flow capacity of the secondaries, watch it! 350 horsepower jump to it, like *now!*

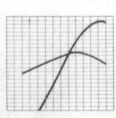

Curve "Ahead"

The 4-4-2 peaks at high rpm —5000 for power, 3600 for torque. And you'll never be late because of weight. The pounds per horsepower reading makes light of things . . . down to a remarkable 9.87 to 1 on the low-priced Club Coupe.

Heat Riser Cutoff

Exclusive on the 4-4-2 Tri-Carb. For peak breathing efficiency at the high end, just pull two bolts from the crossover valves on either side of the center carb, rotate the covers 90° and bolt them back down. So simple it's beautiful.

Tri-Carb Option

4-4-2, plus 3 deuces . . . how about that? A 4-4-2 equipped with the new Tri-Carb option puts out 360 horsepower. For normal cruising the center 2-barrel means economy, for passing power the two end 2-barrels cut in. All three carbs feature maximum-flow air cleaners.

IN THE PALM OF YOUR HAND

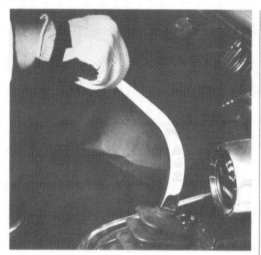

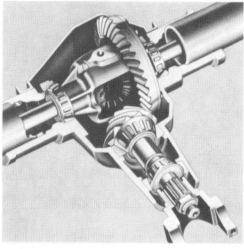

Five for fun

The 4-4-2's geared for it! Name your kind of action. Then pick the transmission that fits. The standard 3-speed column-shift manual has all forward speeds fully synchronized. The snappy floor-mounted version, featuring a Hurst shifter, is a variation. Or you can score with four-on-the-floor. 4-4-2 offers two of 'em. A regular wide-ratio, 4-speed fully synchronzied job has a short-throw Hurst shifter complete with reverse detent. The other is a special close-ratio four-on-the-floor tailored for the real performance enthusiast. And all 4-4-2 manual transmissions share the extra ruggedness of an 11-inch heavy-duty clutch with over 2400 pounds' plate pressure. If you like your action automatic, there's even a special-duty version of Jetaway. This smooth-operating automatic transmission features a variable-vane stator for better performance and economy.

A range of ratios

Eight ways to custom tailor the torque to the rear tires! That's how many rear axle ratios the 4-4-2 offers. They meet virtually any driving need or desire. Factory-installed rear axles come in ratios of 3.23-, 3.55- or 3.90-to-1 with manual transmission . . . and 3.23-, 3.55- or 3.90-to-1 with the special-duty Jetaway. For even more performance, tell your Olds dealer to order 4.11-to-1 . . . or even a 4.33-to-1 ratio. And the Anti-Spin option available on all 4-4-2 rear axles is something else. Provides more drive traction when the going's toughest.

2-Inch Pipes

Another performance feature included with the 4-4-2 option is a special low-restriction exhaust system. The exhaust pipes are a full two inches in diameter to cut down engine back pressure, improve engine breathing.

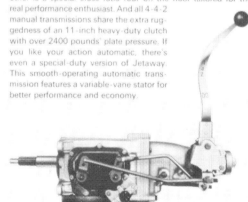

AND THE GOING IS GREAT!

Special Handling

4-4-2 is a moving machine and then some. Oldsmobile didn't stop with power and torque curves . . . the chassis is engineered to make 4-4-2 a stand-out on highway curves. Handling's exceptional. Chassis components are extra rugged. 4-4-2 melts away the miles with its own brand of stamina. You come on *strong* wherever you go in a 4-4-2.

Rugged and Reliable

A car with this kind of action needs more in cooling and electrical equipment. The 4-4-2's heavy-duty radiator and 12-volt, 70-amp.-hr. battery fill the bill with no sweat. The clutch is heavy-duty. So are the propeller shaft . . . front engine mountings . . . and the wheels with extra-wide rims and Red-Line nylon-cord tires.

Steady as She Goes

Front *and rear* stabilizer bars head the list of special 4-4-2 heavy-duty chassis features. The diameter of these bars is 0.937" at the front and 0.875" at the rear. Spring rates on the 4-4-2 are stiffer than normal. Significantly stiffer. With 425 lb./in. front spring rating, the increase is almost 40% . . . with 144 lb./in. rear spring rating, the increase is over 50%. Heavy-duty front and rear shocks, too. They contribute to 4-4-2 stability. Interested in smooth, flat cornering? Who isn't! Check out a 4-4-2 at every turn.

YOU GET MORE OUT OF A 4-4-2 BECAUSE OLDS PUTS MORE INTO IT!

If you think of a sports car as nothing but buckets and baubles, then stop reading. The 4-4-2's not your baby. Sure, of course you can get a 4-4-2 with bucket seats. Nothing wrong with that. But you can also get it as a stripped-down club coupe that gives great performance per dollar. For that's the essence of this machine. Performance.

Take the engine. Precision cast, lightweight. Up to 360 horsepower. Smooth . . . and powerful . . . and beautiful to behold. Or take the chassis. Beefed up . . . even includes a rear stabilizer. Makes rounding curves as smooth as the engine's torque curve.

Built from the road up, 4-4-2's not just to look at and admire. It says get under the hood and listen to it purr. It says get down underneath the chassis to check out the real goods. Most of all, it says get behind the wheel every chance you get.

When 4-4-2 makes the scene, *watch out!*

442 SPECIFICATIONS

ENGINE

GENERAL

Type	90° V-8 Overhead Valve
Horsepower	350 @ 5000 rpm (Quadrajet)
	360 @ 5000 rpm (Tri-Carb)
Torque	440 lb.-ft. @ 3600 rpm
Piston Displacement	400 cu. in.
Bore Spacing	4.625 in. between centers
Bore and Stroke	4.000 x 3.975 in.
Firing Order	1-8-4-3-6-5-7-2
Compression Ratio	10.50 to 1
Cylinder Block and Heads Material	Cast Alloy Iron
Fuel recommended	Premium Gasoline

Idle Speed:
With Manual Transmission .... 600 rpm in Neutral
With Automatic Transmission .... 550 rpm in Drive
Pistons: Aluminum Alloy Autothermic Design with Flat Head and Cam Ground, Tin-Plated, Steel-Strut-Reinforced Skirt
Piston Pins: Pressed in Rod
Connecting Rods: Weight . . . 31.08 oz.; Bearing Type . . . . Steel-Backed Aluminum Moraine 400; Bearing Clearance . . . 0.0005-0.0026 in.
Crankshaft: Material . . . A.I.S.I. #1049 Modified; Vibration Damper . . . Tuned Rubber; End Thrust . . . Taken by #3 Bearing; End Play . . . 0.004-0.008 in.
Main Bearings: Material . . . Steel-Backed Aluminum Moraine 400; Journal Diameter . . . 3.000 in.; Bearing Overall Length . . . 0.975 in. (#1, 2, 4), 1.194 in. (#3), 1.624 in. (#5)
Cylinder Head Volume: 76.00 cc ± 1.00 cc
Cylinder Head Gasket: Thickness . . . 0.023-0.027 in.; Volume . . . 0.326-0.391 cu. in.
Min. Deck Clearance: 0.002 in.
Total Combustion Chamber Volume: 86.29 cc
Carburetor: Type . . . 4-Barrel Quadrajet; Primary Throttle Bore . . . 1.375 in.; Secondary Throttle Bore . . . 2.250 in.
Type . . . Tri-Carb; Center Throttle Bore . . . 1.688 in.; End Throttle Bore . . . 1.688 in.

TIMING

Camshaft: Material . . . Cast Alloy Iron; Bearings . . . 5 Steel-Backed Durex; Drive . . . Chain
Valve Train: Type . . . Independent, for Each Valve; Lifters . . . Hydraulic; Rocker Ratio . . . 1.6 to 1

Valves:	Intake	Exhaust
Max. Head Diameter	2.067 in.	1.629 in.
Seat and Face Angle	30°	45°
Max. Lift	0.472 in.	0.472 in.
Valve Timing:	Intake	Exhaust
Valve Opens	30° BTC	78° BBC
Valve Closes	76° ABC	28° ATC
Duration	286°	286°
Overlap	58°	—

Outer Valve Spring Pressure and Length:	Intake and Exhaust
Valve Closed	84 lb. max. @ 1.670 in.
Valve Open	194 lb. max. @ 1.270 in.

Ignition Timing (crankshaft degrees) . . . 7½° BTC @ 850 rpm
Distributor: Model . . . Delco Remy 1111042; Centrifugal Advance (crankshaft degrees) . . . Start, 0-2° @ 650 rpm; Intermediate Points, 12-16° @ 1800 rpm; Maximum, 20-24° @ 4000 rpm; Breaker Gap . . . 0.016 in.; Cam Angle . . . 28-32°
Coil: Model . . . Delco Remy 1115216—T-3153-A
Spark Plugs: Model . . . AC 44S; Gap . . . 0.030 in.

ELECTRICAL SUPPLY

Battery: Model . . . Delco Remy 1980568; Voltage Rating and No. of Plates . . . 12/77; Ampere-Hour Rating . . . . 70; Terminal Grounded . . . Negative
Delcotron: Model . . . Delco Remy 1100705

COOLING—LUBRICATION—EXHAUST

Cooling: Radiator Cap Relief Valve Pressure . . . . 15 psi; Radiator Core Type . . . Cross Flow; System Capacity with Heater . . . 17.5 qt.
Lubrication: Normal Oil Pressure . . . 30-45 lb. @ 50 mph; Oil Intake . . . . Stationary; Oil Filter . . . Full Flow
Exhaust: Type . . . Dual; Exhaust Pipe Diameter . . . 2 in.; Mufflers . . . Acoustically Tuned, Opened-Up Mufflers without Resonators

TRANSMISSIONS

3-Speed Fully Synchronized: Shift . . . Column Shift Std., Hurst Floor Shift Opt.; Gear Ratios . . . First 2.42-to-1, Second 1.61-to-1, Third 1.00-to-1, Reverse 2.33-to-1.

4-Speed Fully Synchronized: Shift . . . Hurst Floor Shift; Wide Gear Ratios . . . First 2.52-to-1, Second 1.88-to-1, Third 1.46-to-1, Fourth 1.00-to-1, Reverse 2.60-to-1; Close Gear Ratios . . . First 2.20-to-1, Second 1.64-to-1, Third 1.28-to-1, Fourth 1.00-to-1, Reverse 2.27-to-1.
NOTE: A Close-Ratio Transmission is recommended with rear axle ratios of 3.90-to-1 and higher.

Clutch (Manual Transmissions): Pressure Plate Springs . . . Flat—2450 lbs.; Effective Plate Pressure . . . 2450 lbs.; Clutch Facing Thickness . . . 0.150 in.; Clutch Facing Outside and Inside Dia. . . . 11.0 x 6.5 in.

Special-Duty Jetaway Automatic: Shift . . . Column Shift; Floor Shift Available with Opt. Sports Console; Gear Ratios . . . Low 1.76-to-1, High 1.00-to-1, Reverse 1.76-to-1.

REAR AXLES

Factory-Installed Axle Ratios: With 3-Speed Manual Transmission . . . 3.23-to-1, 3.55-to-1, 3.90-to-1*; With 4-Speed Manual Transmission . . . 3.55-to-1, 3.90-to-1*; With Jetaway Transmission . . . 3.23-to-1, 3.55-to-1, 3.90-to-1*.

Dealer-Installed Axle Ratios: Part No. 9780491 . . . . 4.11-to-1; Part No. 9780492 . . . 4.33-to-1. NOTE: If a 4.11-to-1 or 4.33-to-1 ratio is to be dealer-installed, the buyer should order a 3.55-to-1 or 3.90-to-1 axle from the factory.
*All ratios available with Anti-Spin differential.

CHASSIS

Frame Type . . . Open Center, Perimeter Type Guard Beam.

Front Suspension: Type . . . Independent Coil Spring with Counter-Dive; Spring Size . . . 11.4 in. Design Height, 3.60 in. I.D., 121.5 in. Length, 0.650 in. Dia.; Spring Rate . . 425 lb./in.; Wheel Rate . . . 124 lb./in.; Stabilizer . . . Heavy-Duty Bar, SAE 1070 Material, 0.937 in. Dia.

Rear Suspension: Type . . . Coil-Spring, Heavy-Duty, Four Link, Twin Triangle; Spring Size . . . 8.52 in. Design Height, 5.50 in. I.D., 0.560 in. Dia.; Spring Rate . . . 144 lb./in.; Wheel Rate . . . 130 lb./in.; Stabilizer . . . Heavy-Duty Bar, SAE 1070 Material, 0.875 in. Dia.

Brakes: Type . . . Self-Energizing, Self-Adjusting; Drum Type . . . Centrifugal Cast Iron; Lining Area . . . 155.6 sq. in.; Drum Diameter . . . 9.5 in.

Steering: Type . . . Ball Nut; Gear Ratio . . . 24.0-to-1 Manual; 20.0-to-1 Heavy-Duty Manual; 17.5-to-1 Power Steering; Turning Diameter . . . 41.0 ft.

WEIGHT

	Shipping Weight (lbs.)	Pounds per Horsepower
Club Coupe	3454	9.87
Deluxe Holiday Coupe	3502	10.01
Cutlass Sports Coupe	3506	10.02
Cutlass Holiday Coupe	3523	10.07
Cutlass Convertible	3629	10.37

STANDARD FEATURES

4-4-2 Grille • 4-4-2 Emblems • 4-4-2 Front Fender Vents • 4-4-2 Taillamps and Rear Panel • 4-4-2 Performance V-8 Engine • Heavy-Duty Fully Synchronized 3-Speed Manual Transmission • Heavy-Duty Clutch with Manual Transmission • Heavy-Duty Front and Rear Shock Absorbers • Heavy-Duty Front and Rear Springs • Heavy-Duty Front and Rear Stabilizer Bars • Heavy-Duty Radiator • Heavy-Duty Propeller Shaft • Heavy-Duty Front Engine Mountings • Heavy-Duty Battery • Oversize Dual Exhaust • Heavy-Duty Wheels (14 x 6K Rim)[1] • 7.75 x 14″ Red-Line Nylon-Cord Tires[2]

(1) If chrome wheels (N98) are ordered, regular 14″ wheels are furnished.
(2) If whitewall tires (P26) are ordered, 7.75 x 14″ rayon-cord tires are furnished.

OLDSMOBILE DIVISION

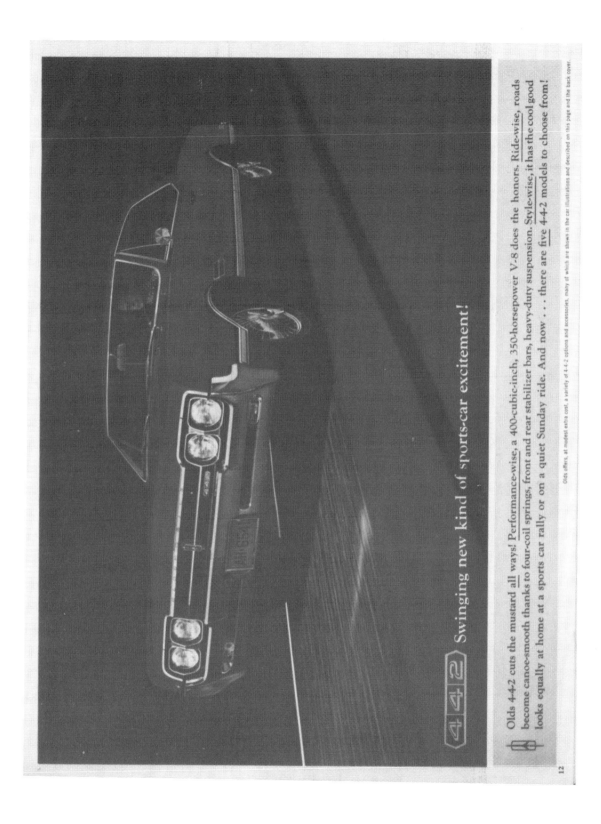

4-4-2 Swinging new kind of sports-car excitement!

Olds 4-4-2 cuts the mustard all ways! Performance-wise, a 400-cubic-inch, 350-horsepower V-8 does the honors. Ride-wise, roads become canoe-smooth thanks to four-coil springs, front and rear stabilizer bars, heavy-duty suspension. Style-wise, it has the cool good looks equally at home at a sports car rally or on a quiet Sunday ride. And now . . . there are five 4-4-2 models to choose from!

Olds offers, at modest extra cost, a variety of 4-4-2 options and accessories, many of which are shown in the car illustrations and described on this page and the back cover.

1966

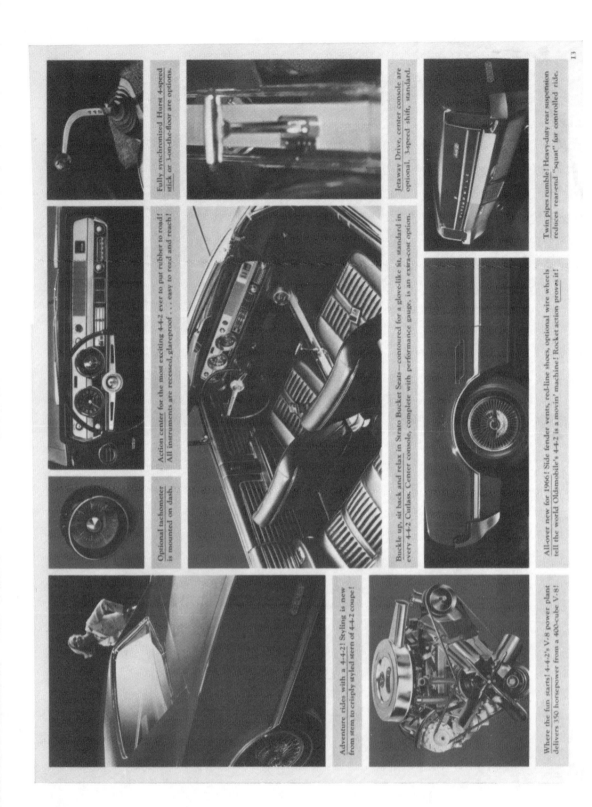

26

4-4-2 PERFORMANCE PACKAGE

New 4-4-2 Cutlass Convertible, like all 4-4-2s, is identified from the sides by fender vents, 4-4-2 emblem, Red-Line tires.

Models available with 4-4-2 equipment include the F-85 Deluxe Holiday Coupe in addition to the standard F-85 Club Coupe and Cutlass Sports Coupe, Holiday Coupe and Convertible.

New and improved, the 4-4-2 Performance Package gives every 4-4-2 great response . . . smooth sports-car handling . . . a distinctive look of its own. Start where the action is—in the 400-cubic-inch block where 350 horsepower helps put 4-4-2 out front. Big manifolds, valves and a new Quadrajet 4-barrel carburetor come along for the ride. And the ride is a great one! A durable propeller shaft transmits the torque to a special performance axle and heavy-duty wheels with extra-wide rims. Low, wide Red-Line tires. Heavy-duty springs, shocks . . . stabilizer bars, front and **rear** . . . give the 4-4-2 superb ride and handling. There's even a heavy-duty radiator and a 70-amp.-hr. battery to handle the extra cooling and electrical needs. A heavy-duty transmission and clutch give the power train extra strength. Add the final touch . . . special 4-4-2 styling and then there's no doubt about it. This is **the** one . . . 4-4-2!

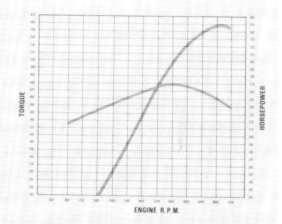

The 4-4-2 Performance V-8 has a cylinder block all its own. The bore is 4.000 inches, the stroke 3.975 inches. Compression ratio is 10.50 to 1. At 5000 rpm, the engine develops 350 horsepower. And torque is 440 pound-feet at 3600 rpm.

Simply styled taillamps help distinguish 4-4-2s from the rear.

A special grille and plain hood identify 4-4-2s from the front.

4-4-2 Deluxe Holiday Coupe ... MODEL 3617*

*With 4-4-2 Performance Package

CHASSIS FEATURES

★ 4-4-2 Performance V-8 Engine with Dual Exhausts
★ Heavy-Duty Radiator
★ 70-Ampere-Hour Battery
■ Heavy-Duty Clutch
■ Heavy-Duty Fully Synchronized 3-Speed Manual Transmission
★ Heavy-Duty Propeller Shaft
★ Red-Line Nylon Tires on H.D. Wheels

Self-Adjusting Brakes
Foot-Operated Parking Brake
Guard-Beam Frame
★ Heavy-Duty Front Engine Mountings
★ Heavy-Duty Front and Rear Suspension

EXTERIOR FEATURES

Recessed Rear Window
Curved Glass Side Windows

Left-Hand Outside Rearview Mirror
Windshield Washer and 2-Speed Wipers with Glare-Resistant Arms and Blades
Windshield, Rear Window, Roof Drip, Rocker Panel, Rear Fender and Wheel Opening Mouldings
★ 4-4-2 Grille and Fender Vents
★ 4-4-2 Taillamps and Rear Panel
Dual Back-Up Lamps
★ 4-4-2 Emblems

★ *Special feature of this model.*   ■ *Standard equipment that costs extra in other Oldsmobile models.*

4-4-2 Club Coupe ... MODEL 3407*

*With 4-4-2 Performance Package

CHASSIS FEATURES

★ 4-4-2 Performance V-8 Engine with Dual Exhausts
★ Heavy-Duty Radiator
★ 70-Ampere-Hour Battery
■ Heavy-Duty Clutch
■ Heavy-Duty Fully Synchronized 3-Speed Manual Transmission
★ Heavy-Duty Propeller Shaft

★ Red-Line Nylon Tires on H.D. Wheels
Self-Adjusting Brakes
Foot-Operated Parking Brake
Guard-Beam Frame
★ Heavy-Duty Front Engine Mountings
★ Heavy-Duty Front and Rear Suspension

EXTERIOR FEATURES

Recessed Rear Window
Curved Glass Side Windows

Windshield Washer and 2-Speed Wipers with Glare-Resistant Arms and Blades
Left-Hand Outside Rearview Mirror
Windshield and Rear Window Mouldings
★ 4-4-2 Grille, Fender Vents, Taillamps and Rear Panel
Dual Back-Up Lamps
★ 4-4-2 Emblems

★ *Special feature of this model.*   ■ *Standard equipment that costs extra in other Oldsmobile models.*

400-CU.-IN.
V-8 ENGINE

4-4-2 Performance V-8
also features Quadrajet!

The 4-4-2 Performance V-8 was specifically developed to give Oldsmobile 4-4-2 models extra performance with durability and dependability to match.

High compression, Fire-Swirl combustion chambers, big valves and manifolds and full dual exhausts give the engine deep breathing ability for the most efficient performance. And the efficiency is improved by the addition of Oldsmobile's new Quadrajet carburetor. (See page 74.)

In other respects, the engine matches the Super Rockets, feature for feature, providing dependable performance in all phases of its operation.

More important is the engine's "square" design (nearly equal bore and stroke) that results in its 400-cubic-inch displacement. This balances the performance with equal stamina.

The engine is the most important component of the 4-4-2 Performance Package. Other components include heavy-duty chassis units with corresponding durability and dependability to assure top performance of the 4-4-2s.

4-4-2 SPECIFICATIONS

ENGINE

GENERAL

Type .... 90° V-8 Overhead Valve
Horsepower .... 350 @ 5000 rpm
Torque .... 440 lb.-ft. @ 3600 rpm
Piston Displacement .... 400 cu. in.
Bore Spacing .... 4.625 in. between centers
Bore and Stroke .... 4.000 x 3.975 in.
Firing Order 1-8-4-3-6-5-7-2
Compression Ratio .... 10.50 to 1
Cylinder Block and Heads Material ...... Cast Alloy Iron
Fuel recommended .... Premium Gasoline
Idle Speed:
   With Manual Transmission .... 600 rpm in Neutral
   With Automatic Transmission .... 500 rpm in Drive

Pistons: Aluminum Alloy Autothermic Design with Flat Head and Cam Ground, Tin-Plated, Steel-Strut-Reinforced Skirt

Piston Pins: Pressed in Rod

Connecting Rods: Weight ... 31.08 oz.; Bearing Type ... Steel-Backed Aluminum Moraine 400; Bearing Clearance ... 0.0005-0.0026 in.

Crankshaft: Material ... A.I.S.I. #1049 Modified; Vibration Damper ... Tuned Rubber; End Thrust ... Taken by #3 Bearing; End Play ... 0.004-0.008 in.

Main Bearings: Material ... Steel-Backed Aluminum Moraine 400; Journal Diameter ... 3.000 in.; Bearing Overall Length ... 0.975 in. (#1, 2, 4), 1.194 in. (#3), 1.624 in. (#5)

Cylinder Head Volume: 76.00 cc ± 1.00 cc

Cylinder Head Gasket: Thickness ... 0.023-0.027 in.; Volume ... 0.326-0.391 cu. in.

Min. Deck Clearance: 0.014 in.

Total Combustion Chamber Volume: 86.29 cc

Carburetor: Type ... 4-Barrel Quadrajet; Primary Throttle Bore ... 1.375 in.; Secondary Throttle Bore ... 2.250 in.

TIMING

Camshaft: Material ... Cast Alloy Iron; Bearings ... 5 Steel-Backed Durex; Drive ... Chain

Valve Train: Type ... Independent, for Each Valve; Lifters ... Hydraulic; Rocker Ratio ... 1.6 to 1

Valves:	Intake	Exhaust
Max. Head Diameter	2.067 in.	1.629 in.
Seat and Face Angle	30°	45°
Max. Lift	0.472 in.	0.472 in.

Valve Timing:	Intake	Exhaust
Valve Opens	30° BTC	78° BBC
Valve Closes	76° ABC	28° ATC
Duration	286°	286°
Overlap	58°	—

Outer Valve Spring Pressure and Length:	Intake and Exhaust
Valve Closed	84 lb. max. @ 1.670 in.
Valve Open	194 lb. max. @ 1.270 in.

Ignition Timing (crankshaft degrees) ... 7½° BTC @ 850 rpm

Distributor: Model ... Delco Remy 1111042; Centrifugal Advance (crankshaft degrees) ... Start, 0-2° @ 650 rpm; Intermediate Points, 12-16° @ 1800 rpm; Maximum, 20-24° @ 4000 rpm; Breaker Gap ... 0.016 in.; Cam Angle ... 28-32°

Coil: Model ... Delco Remy 1115216—T-3153-A

Spark Plugs: Model ... AC 44S; Gap ... 0.030 in.

ELECTRICAL SUPPLY

Battery: Model ... Delco Remy 1980568; Voltage Rating and No. of Plates ... 12/77; Ampere-Hour Rating ... 70; Terminal Grounded ... Negative

Delcotron: Model ... Delco Remy 1100705

COOLING—LUBRICATION—EXHAUST

Cooling: Radiator Cap Relief Valve Pressure ... 15 psi; Radiator Core Type ... Cross Flow; System Capacity with Heater ... 17.5 qt.

Lubrication: Normal Oil Pressure ... 30-45 lb. @ 50 mph; Oil Intake ... Stationary; Oil Filter ... Full Flow

Exhaust: Type ... Dual; Exhaust Pipe Diameter ... 2 in.; Mufflers ... Acoustically Tuned, Opened-Up Mufflers without Resonators

TRANSMISSIONS

3-Speed Fully Synchronized: Shift ... Column Shift Std., Hurst Floor Shift Opt.; Gear Ratios ... First 2.42 to 1, Second 1.61 to 1, Third 1.00 to 1, Reverse 2.33 to 1.

4-Speed Fully Synchronized: Shift ... Hurst Floor Shift; Wide Gear Ratios ... First 2.52 to 1, Second 1.88 to 1, Third 1.46 to 1, Fourth 1.00 to 1, Reverse 2.60 to 1; Close Gear Ratios ... First 2.20 to 1, Second 1.64 to 1, Third 1.28 to 1, Fourth 1.00 to 1, Reverse 2.27 to 1.
NOTE: A Close-Ratio Transmission is recommended with rear axle ratios of 3.90 to 1 and higher.

Clutch (Manual Transmissions): Pressure Plate Springs ... Flat—2450 lbs.; Effective Plate Pressure ... 2450 lbs.; Clutch Facing Thickness ... 0.150 in.; Clutch Facing Outside and Inside Dia. ... 11.0 x 6.5 in.

Special-Duty Jetaway Automatic: Shift ... Column Shift; Floor Shift Available with Opt. Sports Console; Gear Ratios ... Low 1.76 to 1, High 1.00 to 1, Reverse 1.76 to 1

REAR AXLES

Factory-Installed Axle Ratios: With 3-Speed Manual Transmission ... 3.23 to 1, 3.55 to 1, 3.90 to 1*; With 4-Speed Manual Transmission ... 3.55 to 1, 3.90 to 1*; With Jetaway Transmission ... 3.23 to 1, 3.55 to 1, 3.90 to 1*

Dealer-Installed Axle Ratios: Part No. 9780491 ... 4.11 to 1; Part No. 9780492 ... 4.33 to 1. NOTE: If a 4.11 to 1 or 4.33 to 1 ratio is to be dealer-installed, the buyer should order a 3.55 to 1 or 3.90 to 1 axle from the factory.

*All ratios available with Anti-Spin differential.

CHASSIS

Frame Type ... Open Center, Perimeter Type Guard-Beam

Front Suspension: Type ... Independent Coil Spring with Counter-Dive; Spring Size ... 11.4 in. Design Height, 3.60 in. I.D., 121.5 in. Length, 0.650 in. Dia.; Spring Rate ... 425 lb./in.; Wheel Rate ... 124 lb./in.; Stabilizer ... Heavy-Duty Bar, SAE 1070 Material, 0.937 in. Dia.

Rear Suspension: Type ... Coil-Spring, Heavy-Duty, Four Link, Twin Triangle; Spring Size ... 8.52 in. Design Height, 5.50 in. I.D., 0.560 in. Dia.; Spring Rate ... 144 lb./in.; Wheel Rate ... 130 lb./in.; Stabilizer ... Heavy-Duty Bar, SAE 1070 Material, 0.875 in. Dia.

Brakes: Type ... Self-Energizing, Self-Adjusting; Drum Type ... Centrifugal Cast Iron; Lining Area ... 155.6 sq. in.; Drum Diameter ... 9.5 in.

Steering: Type ... Ball Nut; Gear Ratio ... 24.0 to 1 Manual; 20.0 to 1 Heavy-Duty Manual; 17.5 to 1 Power Steering; Turning Diameter ... 41.0 ft.

WEIGHT

	Shipping Weight (lbs.)	Pounds per Horsepower
Club Coupe	3454	9.87
Deluxe Holiday Coupe	3502	10.01
Cutlass Sports Coupe	3506	10.02
Cutlass Holiday Coupe	3523	10.07
Cutlass Convertible	3629	10.37

STANDARD FEATURES (L78)

4-4-2 Grille • 4-4-2 Emblems • 4-4-2 Front Fender Vents • 4-4-2 Taillamps and Rear Panel • 4-4-2 Performance V-8 Engine • Heavy-Duty Fully Synchronized 3-Speed Manual Transmission • Heavy-Duty Clutch with Manual Transmission • Heavy-Duty Front and Rear Shock Absorbers • Heavy-Duty Front and Rear Springs • Heavy-Duty Front and Rear Stabilizer Bars • Heavy-Duty Radiator • Heavy-Duty Propeller Shaft • Heavy-Duty Front Engine Mountings • Heavy-Duty Battery • Oversize Dual Exhaust • Heavy-Duty Wheels (14 x 6K Rim)[1] • 7.75 x 14" Red-Line Nylon Tires[2]

(1) If chrome wheels (N98) are ordered, regular 14" wheels are furnished.
(2) If whitewall tires (P26) are ordered, 7.75 x 14" rayon cord tires are furnished.

For this model year, Oldsmobile dropped a couple of slots in the industry sales race. A total of 548,390 sales brought the division into sixth place. Despite the sales lag, the Cutlass/F-85 group continued to play a more prominent role in the Olds sales mix and the optionally equipped high performance cars were well received. A total of 24,833 4-4-2s were built.

In 1967, the optional 4-4-2 package was number L-78 and this year it could only be ordered on a Cutlass Supreme sports coupe, holiday coupe or convertible. Factory ordering literature indicates the 4-4-2 could not be had as an F-85 or Cutlass model. The $184 L-78 (or 4-4-2) package included a special 350 hp Rocket V-8 engine, F-70x14 wide-tread, redline nylon cord tires, heavy-duty suspension components, special 4-4-2 emblems and dual exhausts. The best horsepower-to-weight ratio was found on the 3,452 pound sports coupe at 9.86 pounds per hp.

A variety of high performance options were found in the Olds dealer book this year. They included: K-66, the $100 transistorized ignition system; U-21, the $84 Rocket Rally pack which consisted of tachometer, electric clock, ammeter, oil pressure and temperature gauge; PO-5, the $88 Super Stock wheels; J-52, the $104 power front disc brakes; and G-80, the $42 anti-spin rear axle.

In 1967, Oldsmobile began tagging its performance options with the "W" prefix. Part number 230309 was alternately known as the W-30 package. It was only sold as a dealer installed option. The package also was tagged the "outside air induction system." It was available only on 4-4-2-optioned Cutlass Supremes. Package parts included a special fan shroud, air duct, special camshaft and heavy-duty valve springs. To allow room for the air ducts and to offer better weight distribution the battery was moved to the trunks. Chrome valve covers and a chrome air cleaner completed the package.

If going fast was on the minds of 4-4-2 option buyers, going further on a tankful of gas appealed to a few other Cutlass Supreme buyers, and Olds was exploring ways to respond to the needs of various special interest car buyers. Option L-66 was the $142 turnpike cruising option, and was sort of a detuned 4-4-2 designed specifically for long-range cruising. It consisted of a 300 hp Rocket 400 cid V-8 that sipped fuel through a two-barrel carburetor. The package also used a "climatic combustion air induction system," 7.75x14 whiteline nylon tires and heavy-duty chassis items. A Turbo-Hydramatic transmission had to be ordered.

Again in 1967, the 4-4-2 was accorded its own four-page color folder. It outlined the 4-4-2 equipment and other performance options (see pages 32-35).* The performance cars were not ignored in the full-line printed offerings from Olds this year, either. The 4-4-2 option was accorded two full pages in the full-line color catalogue (see pages 36-37).* The Vol. 12, No. 4 issue of the "Oldsmobile Rocket Circle" magazine included an interesting 4-4-2 page in this issue, which was titled, "Youth and the Oldsmobile..." (see page 36).*

*Front covers shown below.

MEET THE CAR THAT OLDS BUILDS FOR PEOPLE ON THE _GO_

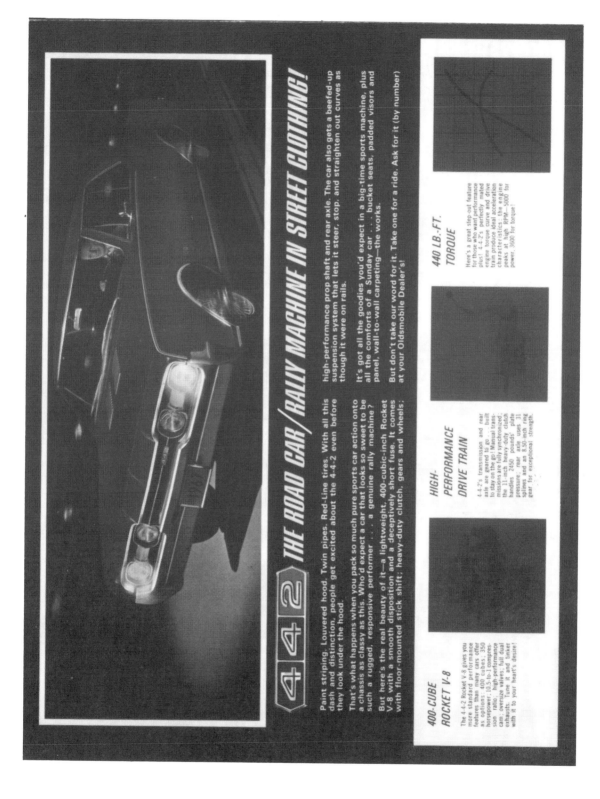

442

THE ROAD CAR/RALLY MACHINE IN STREET CLOTHING!

Paint striping. Louvered hood. Twin pipes. Red-Line tires. With all this dash and distinction, people get excited about the 4-4-2 even before they look under the hood.

That's what happens when you pack so much pure sports car action onto a chassis as classy as this. Who'd expect a car that looks so sweet to be such a rugged, responsive performer . . . a genuine rally machine?

But here's the real beauty of it—a lightweight, 400-cubic-inch Rocket V-8 with a smooth disposition and a deceptively short fuse. It comes with floor-mounted stick shift; heavy-duty clutch, gears and wheels;

high-performance prop shaft and rear axle. The car also gets a beefed-up suspension system that lets it steer, stop, and straighten out curves as though it were on rails.

It's got all the goodies you'd expect in a big-time sports machine, plus all the comforts of a Sunday car . . . bucket seats, padded visors and panel, wall-to-wall carpeting—the works.

But don't take our word for it. Take one for a ride. Ask for it (by number) at your Oldsmobile Dealer!

400-CUBE ROCKET V-8

The 4-4-2 Rocket V-8 gives you more standard performance features than many cars offer as optionals: 400 cubes, 350 horsepower, 10.5-to-1 compression ratio, high-performance cam, oversize valves, full dual exhausts. Tune it and tinker with it to your heart's desire!

HIGH-PERFORMANCE DRIVE TRAIN

4-4-2's transmission and rear axle are geared to go . . . built to stay on the go. Manual transmissions are fully synchronized; the 11-inch heavy-duty clutch handles 2450 pounds' plate pressure; rear axle uses 31 splines and an 8.50-inch ring gear for exceptional strength.

440 LB.-FT. TORQUE

Here's a great step-out feature for those who want performance plus. 4-4-2's perfectly mated engine-torque curve and drive train produce ideal acceleration characteristics. The engine peaks at high RPM—5000 for power, 3600 for torque!

442 OPTIONS AND ACCESSORIES

FROM DISC BRAKES TO UHV, GO THE LIMIT IN PERFORMANCE EQUIPMENT !

A. UHV Transistorized Ignition System— Eliminates breaker points and condenser of standard ignition. Improves performance, minimizes tune-ups and timing adjustments, permits use of a variety of plug gaps without power loss.

B. Rocket Rally Pac— Compact instrument cluster lets driver monitor engine performance at a glance. Includes tachometer, electric clock, ammeter, oil pressure and temperature gauges.

C. Super Stock Wheels— Husky competition-styled wheels feature polished chrome trim rings and wheel nuts, 5-spoke "spiders." Slotted vents draw in air, help cool brakes.

D. Power Front Disc Brakes— Recommended for strenuous driving and severe braking. Advantages are excellent straight-line stopping, consistent pedal feel and long lining life.

E. 4-4-2 Turbo Hydra-Matic— Specially built for high-performance usage and perfectly mated to the 4-4-2 engine. Two automatic torque-boosting actions make passing, maneuvering faster and easier. This transmission may be downshifted at any time when resulting RPM does not exceed 5200.

F. Four-Speed Fully Synchronized Transmission— Available with standard or special fast-shifting gear ratios. Helical-cut, forged steel gears are fully synchronized in all forward speeds. Teams with Hurst shifter for maximum control of engine car speed.

G. Anti-Spin Rear Axle— Automatically directs power to the wheel with the most traction. Provides positive traction in snow, ice, mud, sand. Available in a variety of ratios.

Force-Air-Induction System (Olds Part No. 230309)— Recommended for sustained high-performance. Cold air is drawn in from scoops above and below parking lights, routed through pressure tubes to produce ram effect in carburetor. Includes high-capacity air cleaner. Battery is mounted in trunk. (Dealer-installed only.)

A FULL HOUSE OF PERFORMANCE FEATURES... STANDARD ON 4-4-2!

QUADRAJET 4-BARREL CARBURETOR— Quadrajet design features small primary bores for cruising economy when you want it. For big capacity secondaries for peak power when you need it.

WIDE RANGE OF AXLE RATIOS— Oldsmobile's 4-4-2 offers a raft of axle ratios, factory-installed, include 3.08, 3.23, 3.55, and 3.90-to-1 at no extra cost—plus 3.42 and 3.91-to-1 performance gears with heavy-duty shafts, bearings and differential gears. (Optional dealer-installed ratios of 4.11- and 4.33-to-1 also are available at extra cost.)

HURST SHIFTER—Floor-mounted Hurst Competition Shifter is teamed with 3-speed and 4-speed fully-synchronized manual transmission. Short-throw design and narrow pattern across neutral put more action in the palm of your hand!

HEAVY-DUTY SUSPENSION—4-4-2's special suspension system includes sway bars front and rear, high-rate coil springs and heavy-duty shock absorbers. The result is a smooth, stable ride, flat cornering, more positive control in every driving situation!

442 SPECIFICATIONS

3 VARIATIONS ON THE SAME SWINGING THEME!

442 HOLIDAY COUPE

442 SPORTS COUPE

442 CONVERTIBLE

OLDSMOBILE RESERVES THE RIGHT TO MAKE CHANGES AT ANY TIME, WITHOUT NOTICE, IN PRICES, COLORS, MATERIALS, EQUIPMENT, SPECIFICATIONS AND MODELS, AND ALSO TO DISCONTINUE MODELS.

GM
MARK OF EXCELLENCE

OLDSMOBILE DIVISION

ENGINE

Type .... 90° V-8 Overhead Valve
Horsepower .... 350 @ 5000 rpm (350 @ 5400 rpm with Force-Air Induction System — W30 option)

Torque .... 440 lb.-ft. @ 3600 rpm (440 @ 4000 rpm with W30 option)

Piston Displacement .... 400 cu. in.
Bore Spacing .... 4.625 in. between centers
Bore and Stroke ...... 3.988 x 3.975 in.
Compression Ratio .... 10.5 to 1
Cylinder Block and Head Material ... Cast Alloy Iron
Fuel Recommended and Tank Capacity ... Premium Gasoline 20 gal.
Idle Speed:
  With Manual Transmission ... 600 rpm in Neutral
  With Automatic Transmission ... 550 rpm in Drive
Pistons, Aluminum Alloy Autothermic Design with Flat Head and Cam Ground
Tin-Plated, Steel Strut Reinforced Skirt
Piston Pins Pressed-in Rod
Connecting Rods, Weight .... Steel-Backed
Bearing Material .... Babbitt Lined
Crankshaft, Material .... Steel-Backed Aluminum
Rubber End Thrust ... Taken by #3 Bearing, End Play
Main Bearings, Material ... Steel-Backed Aluminum
Diameter .... 3.000 in., Bearing Overall Length
Cylinder Head Volume ... 75.00 cc (min. 71.9)
Cylinder Head Gasket, Thickness ... 0.023-0.027 in.
Carburetor, Type ... 4-barrel Quadrajet, Primary Throttle Bore
Secondary Throttle Bore ... 2.250 in.

TIMING

Camshaft, Material .... Cast Alloy Iron
Bearings M195, Drive .... Chain
Valve Lifters, Type ... Independent for each Valve
Rocker Ratio .... 1.6 to 1
Valves:
  Max. Head Diameter
  Seat and Face Angle
  Max. Lift
Valve Timing
Valve Opens
Valve Closes
Variation
Outer Valve Spring Pressure and Length
Valve Closed
Valve Open
Ignition Timing (crankshaft degrees)
Distributor, Model ... Delco-Remy 1111188, Centrifugal Advance (crankshaft degrees)
Coil, Model .... Delco-Remy 1115076, Cam Angle
Spark Plugs, Model ... AC 445, Gap
NOTE: UHV (Ultra High Voltage) Transistorized Ignition System Available.

ELECTRICAL SUPPLY

Battery, Model ... Delco-Remy 1980038, Voltage Rating and No. of Plates
Generator, Model ... Delco-Remy 30 Terminal Grounded ... Negative

COOLING-LUBRICATION-EXHAUST

Cooling System, Capacity with Heater
Lubrication System, Capacity
Stationary, Oil Filter, Full Flow
Exhaust, Type ... Dual, Exhaust Pipe Diameter ... 2.25 in., Mufflers ...
Acoustically Tuned, Straight Through Mufflers and Resonators

TRANSMISSIONS

3-Speed Fully Synchronized, Shift ... Heavy Floor Shift, Gear Ratios
4-Speed, Shift ... Heavy Floor Shift, Wide Gear Ratios
Clutch (Manual Transmission), Pressure Plate Springs
Turbo Hydra-Matic, Shift ... Column Shift, Floor Shift Available with Opt.

REAR AXLES

Factory-Installed Axle Ratios ... With 3-Speed Manual Transmission ... Std.
With Turbo Hydra-Matic Transmission ... Std.
All ratios available with Anti-Spin Differential
Dealer-Installed Axle Ratios, Part No. 9780491

CHASSIS

Wheelbase .... 115 in., Track
Frame Type .... Open Center Perimeter Type Guard Beam
Front Suspension, Type ... Independent Coil Spring with Counter Dive
  Spring Size ... Design Height
  Bar, Spring Rate ... Wheel Rate
Heavy-Duty Bar SAE 1070 Material
Rear Suspension, Type ... Coil Springs, Heavy-Duty, Four-Link, Twin-Triangle
Heavy-Duty Bar, SAE 1070 Material, Dia.
Brakes, Type ... Self-Energizing, Self-Adjusting, Dual Master Cylinder
Hydraulic System, Drum Type ... Centrifugal Cast Iron Lining Area
Opt. Front-Wheel Disc Brakes, Rotor Type ... Vented Cast Iron
Steering, Type ... Ball Nut with Energy Absorbing Steering Column, Gear Ratio
Steering, Turning Diameter ... 41.7 ft.

WEIGHT

	Shipping Weight (lb.)	Pounds per Horsepower
442 Sports Coupe	3457	9.86
442 Holiday Coupe	3488	9.91
442 Convertible	3575	10.21

STANDARD FEATURES

442 Grille • 442 Emblems • 442 Louvered Hood • 442 G.T. Paint Stripes on Fenders • 442 Rocket V-8 Engine • Heavy-Duty Fully Synchronized 3-Speed Manual Transmission with Hurst Floor Shift • Heavy-Duty Clutch with Manual Transmission • Heavy-Duty Front and Rear Shock Absorbers • Heavy-Duty Front and Rear Springs • Heavy-Duty Front and Rear Stabilizer Bars • Heavy-Duty Battery • Heavy-Duty Propeller Shaft • Heavy-Duty Front Engine Mountings • Heavy-Duty Battery • Dual Exhausts • Heavy-Duty Wheels • F78 x 14" Wide-Tread Red-Line Nylon-Cord Tires(2)
(1) Super Stock Wheels available.
(2) F78 x 14" White-Line Nylon-Cord Tires available.

Litho in U.S.A.

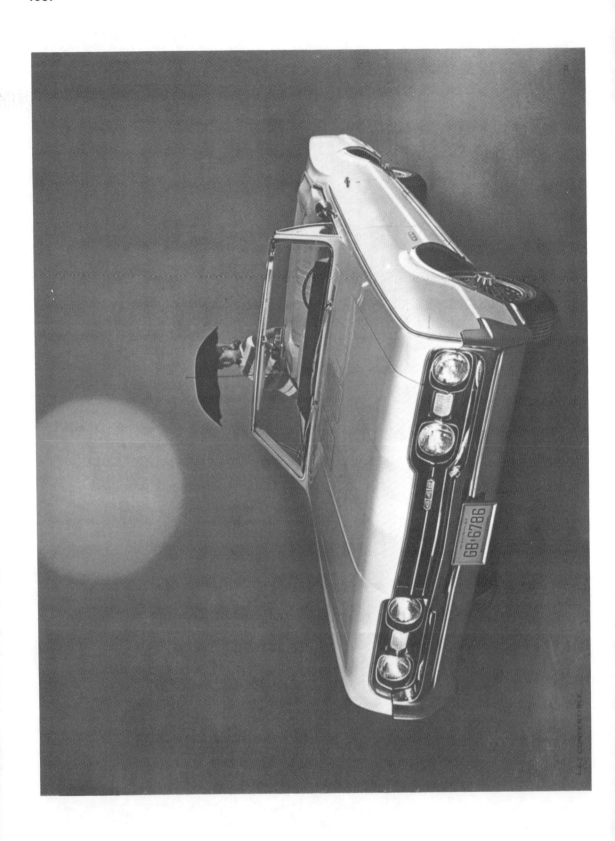

OLDS 4-4-2

Gay blade. Bon vivant. Swashbuckler of the Oldsmobile line.

Every family needs at least one dyed-in-the-wool extrovert. And Olds has three—all called 4-4-2. All genuine-article sports machines. Complete in every detail on a generous 115-inch wheelbase. ◖ Swinging front and rear styling, functionally louvered hood, unique side paint-stripe all set 4-4-2 apart in the looks department. Everything else sets it apart in the action area. ◖ 400-cube 4-4-2 Rocket V-8, for instance—a 350-hp, 4-barrel mill, complete with special cam. High-performance axle. Heavy-duty front and rear suspension. Heavy-duty motor mounts. And heavy-duty wheels with either wide-oval Red-Line or White-Line tires. It's all standard 4-4-2 gear! Inside, buckets are standard (or bench, if you wish). Console (shown left) is also available when you specify Turbo Hydra-Matic Drive or 4-on-the-floor transmission. ◖ Beyond that, you can equip it with goodies galore: new UHV Transistorized Ignition System, front disc brakes, a variety of axle ratios, tach engine gauge are among them. Now who's the swashbuckler in your family? Better tell the whole crew 4-4-2 is here!

4-4-2 SPECIFICATIONS: Wheelbase, 115'; overall length, 204.2'; overall width, 76.0'; overall height 53.6', tire size, F70 x 14". STANDARD EQUIPMENT: 350-hp 4-4-2 Rocket V-8; floor-mounted 3-speed fully synchronized transmission; heavy-duty front and rear suspension; heavy-duty wheels; heavy-duty motor mounts; Red-Line tires; bucket seats; carpeting; heater-defroster; deluxe steering wheel; full complement of Oldsmobile safety features (pages 3 and 45.)

Olds offers, at modest extra cost, a variety of options and accessories, many of which are shown in the car illustrations and described on pages 40, 41 and 46.

4-4-2 HOLIDAY COUPE

4-4-2 SPORTS COUPE

1967 OLDS

**Styled for the
Action Crowd...and
70 Years Young!**

Here's an action mate for a 4-4-2—classic
culotte skirt and rib-knit sweater. '67 yields a
vintage crop, and will be the year sweater
collectors remember! Pleated, flippety, kilty,
dirndl-y—these are the fly-away skirts
of '67. The 4-4-2 is the fly-away car of '67
—another campus favorite. It's revved up
and racy, with flair and fashion.

13

This was a milestone year in the high performance era for Oldsmobile. In its fifth year, the 4-4-2 was upgraded from an option to a full-fledged series within the F-85/Cutlass ranks. Oldsmobile and Hurst Corporation also picked 1968 to produce the first of their special Hurst/Olds creations which offered a unique blend of luxury and high performance for a limited number of buyers. Finally, F-85/Cutlass buyers were offered a completely new body shell and design package this model year. Sales totals of 562,459 enabled Oldsmobile to hang onto sixth place in the industry sales standings for the year.

By an overwhelming margin, the hardtop coupe (model number 4487) was the most popular 4-4-2, with 24,183 made. A total of 4,282 sports (pillared) coupes were made (model number 4477) and 5,142 convertibles (model number 4467) rounded out the new series. The 4-4-2 package was powered by a 400 cid Rocket V-8 which produced 350 hp in stickshift versions and 25 less hp in cars with the Turbo-Hydramatic. A variety of heavy-duty equipment was standard on the series, including: prop shaft and motor mounts, shock absorbers, front and rear stabilizer bars and high rate springs. Heavy-duty wheels were again fitted with redline tires.

The list of performance options available on the 1968 4-4-2 was impressive. It featured: G-88, a no charge 3.91 to 1 rear axle set-up; G-89, a no charge 4.33 to 1 rear axle package; J-52, the $104 power brake unit with front discs; K-66, the $100 high voltage ignition; M-20 (wide-ratio) or M-21 (close-ratio), the $84 special instrumentation Rocket Rally Pac. Again, Olds offered its 290 hp, regular-fueled turnpike cruising option (L-65) which might have been about a decade ahead of its time. In 1968, the W-30 package was continued and centered around a 360 hp, forced air induction motor. The option cost $263.

If an Olds buyer wanted a straight-line performance rocket or something that handled a bit better than most showroom stockers, then it probably could be found somewhere in the 4-4-2 order book. However, if a buyer was concerned with a careful blend of luxury and overall performance—while still staying within the Olds intermediate group—then the new Hurst/Olds was worth a look. Designed initially as a one-off car for performance parts merchandising honcho George Hurst, it quickly became a lim-

ited production offering through selected Olds dealers. Early H/O production was carried out in the Lansing, Michigan, shops of industrialist John Demmer. The 1968 Hurst/Olds could be ordered either as a sports coupe or hardtop coupe. Power came from a special 390 hp, 455 cid Rocket V-8 that was fitted with special heads, camshaft and crankshaft. Other H/O modifications included a modified Turbo-Hydramatic transmission with Hurst Dual Gate shifter, oversize G-70x14 Goodyear polyglass tires, special H/O emblems and interior trim, front disc brakes, heavy-duty suspension components and a high capacity cooling system. For this initial year, all 515 Hurst/Oldses were finished in silver and black.

The 4-4-2 was the lead car in both large and small full-line catalogues put out by Olds in 1968. A total of four pages were devoted to interior and exterior high points of the first-year series (see pages 40-43).* Our cover shot was also part of the overall advertising campaign in 1968. This series featured a number of young people doing adventure-filled things like skydiving (as on the cover shot), mountain climbing, bullfighting, sailing, scuba diving and horseback riding. All shots featured an Oldsmobile superimposed near the adventuresome person or persons. There was surprisingly little printed material on the Hurst/Olds in its inaugural year, but there was a press release and several factory photos, including a shot of an H/O going through the conversion process (see page 44).

*Front cover shown below.

Oldsmobile for '68

4-4-2 Holiday Coupe

4-4-2 is the Youngmobile for the purist. All-new style says so. So do all its goodies. Taut, heavy-duty suspension. 400-cube, 350-hp Rocket V-8. Twin exhausts. Wide-oval Red-Line tires. High-performance axle. Buckets, too.

Hood louvers are very "in" these days, and 4-4-2 makes 'em yours. At no charge.

No denying it: 4-4-2 is quite a show-off—with a whole assortment of ingenious features for being so. Optional extra-cost tach-clock Rocket Rally Pac lets you check the action or check the hour; nestles neatly into instrument panel.

Dual exhausts are standard, too—complete with chrome collars notched into rear bumper.

Fully synchronized 3-on-the-floor gear box is standard. But close- or wide-ratio 4-on-the-floor with Hurst shifter, 3-speed Turbo Hydra-Matic Drive are available at extra cost, too, along with control console.

Wide front-fender Rally Stripe is another 4-4-2 touch you can specify if you care to embellish that rakish new appearance. Included in Oldsmobile's new Force-Air Induction package.

This front-door detailing aptly testifies that austerity has no place in 4-4-2. Vent windows are conveniently crank-operated.

Olds offers, at modest extra cost, a variety of options and accessories, many of which are shown in the car illustrations, and are also described on pages 41, 44 and 45.

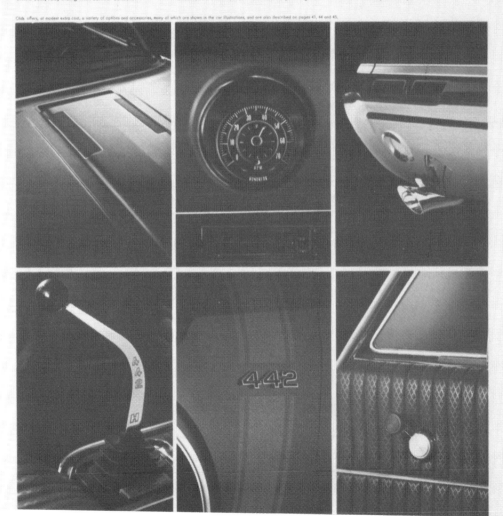

5

4-4-2

What you saw on the previous page would be pizazz aplenty for most cars, but not for 4-4-2! And this dashing dash is just one case in point. Dials are recessed.

You get all kinds of choices when it comes to young wheels. These Custom Sport Wheels, wire wheels or Sport Covers are all available at extra cost. Wide-oval Red-Lines and GT pinstriping are both standard items on 4-4-2.

4-4-2 comes with a pair of these tailored buckets, too (front shoulder belts plus seat belts for all passenger positions included). Bench seat is yours at no charge, if you'd rather have it.

This one's offered purely for the sports addicts: 4-4-2's new-for-'68 Force-Air Induction System. 400-cubic-inch engine that delivers 360 hp, wide range of axle ratios and front-fender Rally Stripe are all part of this package.

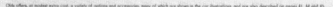

Olds offers, at modest extra cost, a variety of options and accessories, many of which are shown in the car illustrations, and are also described on pages 41, 44 and 45.

4-4-2 Sports Coupe

4-4-2 Convertible

Decisions. Decisions. Just when you'd settled on that Holiday Coupe on the preceding page, up pops 4-4-2 with two more models.

In the performance department they have a 400-CID, four-barrel V-8 that delivers 350 hp, offers greater torque in lower driving ranges. Heavy-duty prop shaft and motor mounts and 3.23-to-1 rear axle are standard. So are high-rate springs and shocks, stabilizers (front and rear) and H.D. wheels with Red-Lines.

If you're strictly a sportsman, front disc brakes and UHV Transistorized Ignition are also available. And 4-4-2's cruising option features a two-barrel V-8 engine and a 2.56-to-1 economy axle.

7

Performance became even more important at Oldsmobile in 1969 and most of that potent automobiling came from the 4-4-2 series. In overall sales standings, Olds moved up a slot to fifth place on the basis of 655,241 sales.

In its second year of full-fledged series status, the 4-4-2 again was available in three basic body styles. Most popular—by far—was the hardtop coupe (model 4487), which was responsible for 19,587 sales. A total of just 2,475 buyers went for the sports (pillared) coupe (model 4477) and 4,295 convertibles (model 4467) were built. The hardtop sold for $3,204, the sports coupe for $3,141 and the convertible for $3,395. Series standard equipment included: a special 400 cid Rocket V-8 engine, 70 amp-hour battery, dual exhausts, hood stripes, Strato bucket seats, heavy-duty suspension components and F-70 red-stripe, wide-oval tires.

The 4-4-2 had become important on the performance horizon in 1969, but this series did not have to carry the Oldsmobile banner alone. The optional status W-cars and the second year Hurst/Oldses were also well received high performance cars from the Olds camp.

The W-car concept could be traced back to 1966 when a handful of specialized W-30 cars were made. By 1968, a potent small block W-31 Cutlass joined the high winding Rocket ranks. For 1969, the W-car line-up was exciting. The W-30 was a forced air induction package feeding a 400 cid, 360 hp Rocket V-8. This 4-4-2 option included special hood striping and W-30 front fender decals. Manditory options here were the anti-spin rear axle and heavy-duty radiator. The W-32 package was a slightly more streetable version of the air inducted 400 cid motor. One source lists its hp at 350, another at 360. Manditory options were the anti-spin rear, heavy-duty radiator and a special Turbo-Hydramatic. The W-31, or as Olds called it, "the Junior Super Car," rounded out the W-team. This option—for the price conscious buyer—could be had on the F-85 sport coupe. It also

was available on the Cutlass S sport and holiday coupes and convertible. It was powered by a forced air induction 325 hp, 350 cid small block V-8.

Olds also offered a special "Ram Rod 350" package for selected Cutlasses. It used the air induction system, a 308 degree hydraulic camshaft and big 455 engine valves set in the small port 350 heads. This was a very limited option.

Satisfied with the basic concept of the 1968 Hurst/Olds, colors were changed and a gold and white H/O was on the scene for 1969. The H/O package was W-46 in the dealer's order book and 906 of the Hurst machines were made. Power on the Hurst/Olds again came from a 455 cid Rocket V-8 turning out a substantial 380 hp. The car had massive air scoops on the hood and a rear spoiler on the trunk. The price was right around $4,300. Other H/O features included a modified Turbo-Hydramatic, Hurst Dual Gate shifter and Goodyear Polyglas tires on seven inch rims. This was one of the few high performance offerings that could be ordered with factory air conditioning.

Oldsmobile was proud of its performance fleet and this showed in its literature for 1969. The Olds advertising agency had developed a Sonny Bono look-alike called Dr. Oldsmobile and he was prominently featured in an eight page black-and-white catalogue on the W-cars (see pages 51-58).* The 4-4-2s rated a four-page section to lead off the intermediate part of the large full-line color catalogue for the year (see pages 46-49).* An interesting and rather rare piece of performance literature was a single folded sheet of light blue paper called, "Dr. Oldsmobile's W Machines." It reviewed the W-30, W-31 and W-32 factory options (see pages 59-60).* The Hurst catalogue was a small, black-and-white-and-gold item (see pages 61-62). An Olds 4-4-2 order blank is also included here (see page 50).

*Front covers shown below.

4-4-2
Makes everything else look tame.

442

How do you match looks like these? There's only one way we know of— and that's with unimpeachable cre-

dentials like these! Special 400-cu.-in. Rocket V8. Special 4-barrel carb. Fully synchronized, heavy-duty transmis-

sion, floor-mounted. High-performance rear end up to 4.66-to-1. Dual low-restriction exhausts. Wide-boot

Oldsmobile recreates a scene from the classic movies.

red-stripe tires. Plus heavy-duty everything underneath it all: H-D shocks, H-D wide-rim wheels, and stabilizer bars—*front and rear*. No other car in 4-4-2's class comes so fully and capably equipped. If you care to, you can order *your* 4-4-2 with a special Force-Air Induction Package with functional dual air scoops.

Some of the equipment illustrated is optional at extra cost.

19

Rocket Rally Pac. Combination tachometer and clock that lets you check your engine performance as you check the time. Package also includes oil-pressure gauge and temperature gauge. Extra cost option.

Give the ordinary the brush-off. Roll on 4-4-2's wide, brushed stainless Custom Sport wheels. Extra cost. Wide-boot Red-Line nylon cords (or whitewalls) on heavy-duty wide-rim wheels, standard.

4-4-2 Convertible with GT Rally Stripes on hood.

Tachometer-clock combination

The sound of music—to a car buff's ear. And if you think this "trumpet" sounds great, wait till you hear the one under 4-4-2's other taillight!

Knob hill. Classy Hurst shifter takes root in 4-4-2's nifty, optional sports console. 4-speed fully synchronized manual (shown) or 3-speed Turbo Hydra-Matic 400 at extra cost. A floor-mounted, fully synchronized, heavy-duty 3-speed manual, standard. And away you go!

New front disc brakes with single piston design, at extra cost. Combine with resized rear drums for improved braking balance, increased durability.

20

Why not order your 4-4-2 Sports Coupe with extra-cost Force-Air Induction? It crams cooler air into the carburetor. Package includes largest air scoops in the business; special air cleaner; special heads and cam; special 2" intake and 1⅝" exhaust ports; and special Dual Hood Stripes. Strictly for the man who has everything.

4-4-2 Sports Coupe

Drop in. You'll land in one of the cushiest buckets ever: 4-4-2's standard Strato Buckets. Well padded, but firm. Carefully contoured for maximum support and comfort. Or you may order a bench seat at no extra cost, if you wish.

Some of the equipment illustrated is optional at extra cost.   21

ZONE COPY
PRINT OF AUG. '68
PRINTED IN U.S.A.

1969 OLDSMOBILE WHOLESALE CAR ORDER
''4-4-2'' MODELS

DATE ORDER RECEIVED AT ZONE (2-4)

DEALER NAME AND ADDRESS	DEALER CODE (16-20)	SETTLEMENT (15)	NUMBER (21-26)	DISTRICT NO. (27)
		A G.M.A.C. C ZONE SETTLEMENT	L17499	
		B O.D.C.—Undersigned dealer certifies that he has current arrangement with an O.D.C. financer and that settlement should be made thru such O.D.C. financer.		

EXTERIOR COLORS (REFERENCE ONLY)

			"C08" VINYL ROOF	CONV. TOP
A—EBONY BLACK	G—TOPAZ	N—BURGUNDY MIST	2—BLACK	1—WHITE
B—SABLE	H—MEADOW GREEN	P—PLATINUM	3—BLUE	2—BLACK
C—CAMEO WHITE	J—AZTEC GOLD	R—CRIMSON	5—PARCHMENT	3—BLUE
D—NASSAU BLUE	K—TAHITIAN TURQUOISE	S—PALOMINO GOLD	8—SABLE	6—GOLD
E—TROPHY BLUE	M—GLADE GREEN	Y—SAFFRON	9—GREEN	

CIRCLE ⬭ BODY STYLE NUMBER, TRIM NUMBER AND COLOR SYMBOL DESIRED

BODY STYLE (28-31)			BLACK VINYL	GREEN VINYL	BLUE VINYL	BLUE CLOTH	GOLD VINYL	GOLD CLOTH	RED VINYL	ANTIQUE PARCH. VINYL	LOWER BODY	ROOF
CONVERTIBLE	STRATO BUCKET FRONT SEATS	4467	30		33		34		35	37	A B C	A B C
	BENCH FRONT SEAT	4467	10	12	13		14			17	D E G	D E G
SPORTS COUPE	STRATO BUCKET FRONT SEAT	4477	30		33		34		35	37	H J K	H J K
	BENCH FRONT SEAT	4477	10	12		43		44		17	M N P	M N P
HOLIDAY COUPE	STRATO BUCKET FRONT SEATS	4487	30		33		34		35	37	R S Y	R S Y
	BENCH FRONT SEAT	4487	10	12		43		44		17		

TRIM (32–33) / COLOR (34–35)

"C08": 2 3 5 8 9   CONV.: 1 2 3 6

ACCESS. GROUPS (36)

37				
1 2				

THERE IS AN OPTION OF RADIOS IN THE GROUP. THE TYPE RADIO DESIRED MUST BE SPECIFIED BY CHECKING THE SYMBOL "U63", "U69" OR "U58"

Group	Sym	Code	Description
37			
39	2	M14	HEAVY-DUTY 3 SPEED FULLY SYNCHRONIZED TRANSMISSION (FLOOR SHIFT)
	3	M20	4 SPEED WIDE RATIO FULLY SYNCHRONIZED TRANSMISSION (FLOOR SHIFT)
	4	M21	4 SPEED CLOSE RATIO FULLY SYNCHRONIZED TRANSMISSION (FLOOR SHIFT - "G80" REQUIRED - "V01" REQUIRED UNLESS "G92" IS ORDERED - "G92" REQUIRES-"V02"-N.A. WITH "C60" OR "Y72")
	7	M40	TURBO HYDRA-MATIC TRANSMISSION 400
40	1	N40	POWER STEERING
	2	J50	POWER BRAKES
	4	JL2	FRONT DISC BRAKES — POWER (N.A. WITH "J50")
41	1	P26	WHITEWALL TIRES
	5	P81	RED STRIPE FIBERGLASS BELTED TIRES
	7	PL5	WIDE OVAL BLACKWALL TIRES WITH WHITE RAISED LETTERS
42	1	P01	WHEEL DISCS
	2	P02	DELUXE WHEEL DISCS
	3	N95	SIMULATED WIRE WHEELS
	4	P05	SUPER STOCK I WHEELS (N.A. WITH "JL2")
	7	N66	SUPER STOCK II WHEELS
43	2	N34	CUSTOM SPORT STEERING WHEEL
	4	N42	DELUXE STEERING WHEEL WITH INSTANT HORN
44	1	N33	TILT-AWAY STEERING COLUMN
	4	C56	FLO-THRU VENTILATION (4477 ONLY-STD. ON 4467 AND 4487)—REQUIRED WITH "C57"-N.A. WITH "C60")
45 U35	1	U35	ELECTRIC CLOCK
A91	2	A91	POWER TRUNK LID LATCH
	4	K30	CRUISE CONTROL ("M40" AND "J50" OR "JL2" REQUIRED)
Y60 Y60	1	Y60	CONVENIENCE GROUP
46 U29	2	U29	COURTESY LAMPS AND MAP LAMP (STD. ON 4467 - INCLUDED ON 4477 AND 4487 WITH "M14", "M20" AND "M21" WHEN "D55" IS ORDERED)
B93 B93	4	B93	DOOR EDGE GUARDS
U63 U63	1	U63	DELUXE PUSHBUTTON RADIO
U69 U69	47 2	U69	AM-FM RADIO
U58 U58	3	U58	AM-FM STEREOPHONIC RADIO AND REAR SEAT SPEAKER

Group	Sym	Code	Description
48	1	U75	POWER ANTENNA (REAR MOUNTED)
	2	U80	REAR SEAT SPEAKER (INCLUDED WITH "U57" AND "U58")
	4	U57	STEREO TAPE PLAYER AND REAR SEAT SPEAKER (RADIO REQUIRED)
49	1	A01	TINTED GLASS
	2	A02	TINTED WINDSHIELD
50	1	C60	AIR CONDITIONER (N.A. WITH "M21", "G88" OR "G92")
	2	V02	HEAVY-DUTY RADIATOR (REQUIRED AND AVAIL. ONLY WITH "G92"-N.A. WITH "C60", "V01" OR "Y72")
	4	Y72	HEAVY-DUTY ENGINE COOLING AND 55 AMP. DELCOTRON (N.A. WITH "M21", "G88", "G92", "V01" OR "V02")
	8	V01	HEAVY-DUTY RADIATOR (REQUIRED AND AVAIL. ONLY WITH "G88"-N.A. WITH "C60", "V02" OR "Y72")
51	1	A39	DELUXE FRONT AND REAR LAP BELTS (4467 ONLY)
	2	AS4	DELUXE REAR SHOULDER BELTS ("A39" OR "W39" REQUIRED)
	4	A85	DELUXE FRONT SHOULDER BELTS (4467 ONLY – "A39" REQUIRED)
	4	W39	DELUXE FRONT AND REAR LAP BELTS AND FRONT SHOULDER BELTS (N.A. ON 4467)
	8	AS5	STANDARD REAR SHOULDER BELTS (N.A. WITH "A39", "A85" OR "W39")
	12	AS1	STANDARD FRONT SHOULDER BELTS (4467 ONLY - N.A. WITH "A39" OR "AS4")
52	2	B32	AUXILIARY FRONT FLOOR MATS
	4	B33	AUXILIARY REAR FLOOR MATS
53	1	U21	ROCKET RALLY PAC (INCLUDES "U35")
	2	U15	SAFETY SENTINEL
	4	D55	SPORT CONSOLE- WITH FLOOR SHIFT (AVAIL. ONLY WITH BUCKET SEATS)
54	1	A31	POWER SIDE WINDOWS
	2	A93	POWER DOOR LOCKS
	4	C57	FORCED AIR VENTILATION ("C56" REQUIRED ON 4477 - N.A. WITH "C60")
55	1	A41	4-WAY POWER BENCH SEAT ADJUSTER
	2	A46	4-WAY POWER BUCKET SEAT ADJUSTER
56	2	M55	AUTOMATIC TRANSMISSION OIL COOLER - AUXILIARY (RECOMMENDED FOR TRAILER TOWING—"M40" REQUIRED)
	4	D33	REMOTE CONTROL OUTSIDE REARVIEW MIRROR
57	1	U89	TRAILER ELECTRICAL WIRING HARNESS
	2	VE1	REAR GUARD RUBBER BUMPER INSERT
	4	G51	HEAVY-DUTY REAR SPRINGS (RECOMMENDED FOR TRAILER TOWING – "M40" REQUIRED)

Group	Sym	Code	Description
58	1	G66	SUPERLIFT REAR SHOCK ABSORBERS (RECOMMENDED FOR TRAILER TOWING "M40" REQUIRED)
	2	G80	ANTI-SPIN REAR AXLE (REQUIRED WITH "G88" OR "G92")
	1	G88	3.91 TO 1 HEAVY-DUTY REAR AXLE ("G80" AND "V01" REQUIRED-N.A. WITH "M20", "C60" OR "Y72")
	3	G90	3.08 TO 1 REAR AXLE RATIO (N.A. WITH "M21")
	4	G91	3.23 TO 1 REAR AXLE RATIO (N.A. WITH "M21")
59	5	G92	3.42 TO 1 HEAVY DUTY REAR AXLE RATIO ("G80" AND "V02" REQUIRED-N.A. WITH "C60" OR "Y72")
	7	G95	2.56 TO 1 REAR AXLE RATIO (AVAIL. ONLY WITH "M40")
	8	G96	2.56 TO 1 EXPRESSWAY AXLE (AVAIL. ONLY WITH "M40")
60		Y73	HOOD G.T. PAINT STRIPE (COLOR SELECTION REQUIRED - RECOMMEND HOOD PAINT STRIPE MATCH ROOF OR INTERIOR TRIM COLOR IF POSSIBLE - COLORS: A-BLACK, C-WHITE, E-BLUE, G-GOLD AND R-RED - INSERT COLOR DESIRED HERE ▸
61	1	W42	DUAL STRIPE HOOD - DELETES "Y73" HOOD G.T. PAINT STRIPE (COLOR SELECTION REQUIRED IN COLUMN 60)
64	1	C50	REAR WINDOW DEFOGGER (N.A. ON 4467)

Dealer Demonstrator	D	Fleet Order	F	Fleet Replacement	W	(VEHICLE IDENTIFICATION NUMBER OF CAR DELIVERED TO FLEET USER)
Retail Order (76)	S					

(CUSTOMER'S NAME)   (ADDRESS)   (DEALER'S SIGNATURE)   (ORDER DATE - 78-80)

511-OLDS
4-4-2

SHADED OPTION SYMBOLS INDICATE ITEM HAS LIMITED USAGE AS NOTED.

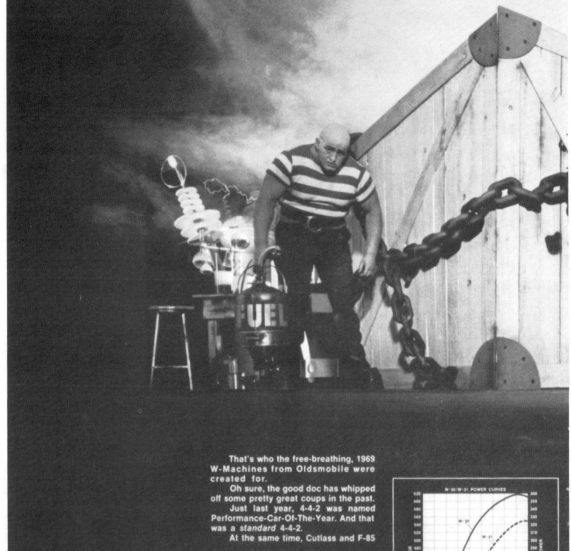

That's who the free-breathing, 1969 W-Machines from Oldsmobile were created for.

Oh sure, the good doc has whipped off some pretty great coups in the past.

Just last year, 4-4-2 was named Performance-Car-Of-The-Year. And that was a *standard* 4-4-2.

At the same time, Cutlass and F-85

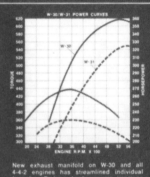

New exhaust manifold on W-30 and all 4-4-2 engines has streamlined individual branches. Reduces back-pressure, improves tuning. New W-30 and W-31 engines feature more usable power through entire speed range. W-Machines' power curves shown.

...BUT IS THE WORLD READY?

A small, sophisticated part of it is.

That small, knowing part that demands a whole lot more out of a set of treads than just transportation.

That small, hard-core part of it that thinks perfection in automobiles is worth shooting for.

That's who the good doctor (and his fanatical engineering sidekicks) pulled on the coveralls for.

How can you tell a W-Machine when you see one? Simple. Just look for a pair of mammoth functional air scoops mounted under the front bumper!

models with newly tooled Rocket 350 V-8s were nailing down honors in the new mini-cube market.

So much for past history.

This year, Dr. Oldsmobile has out-done himself—with a pair of 1969 Ws that are really something else.

Take the new Olds 4-4-2 W-30. That means with Force-Air Induction. And that means with a pair of mammoth front air-scoopers; wide-throat dual air ducts; dual intake air cleaner; minimum combustion chamber volume; separated center exhaust ports for optimum tuning; big intake and exhaust valves; streamlined and individually branched exhaust manifold; high-overlap cam; low-restriction dual exhausts; and a pair of whopper hood paint patches.

Not to mention a multitudinous array of axle ratios. Plus enough standard heavy-duty goodies to make any red-blooded car buff pop a few buttons with honest pride.

And what goes for W-30, goes ditto (in most cases) for its mini-cube mate, W-31. Available in Cutlass S and F-85 V-8 models.

The W-Machines have got it all— looks, swagger, and credentials!

But enough of words. Let's get to the goods.

Turn the page.

And make friends with a 1969 W-Machine. Or two.

Cutaway shot of new floating-caliper-type front power disc brake. Single-piston design. Internal cooling fins rapidly dissipate heat. Availability depending on engine choice.

An inside look at one of eight, beefy, 1969 rear axles. Ratios range all the way to 4.66-to-1. And each and everyone of them is available with limited slip.

1969

DON'T THROW AWAY THE LUMBER. YOU'LL NEED IT TO CRATE UP AND CART OFF THE COMPETITION. OLDS 4-4-2 W-30

W-30 is more than just a great machine. It's a labor of love.

Every moving, breathing part in its engine is individually selected. And matched. And fitted. To extremely close tolerances.

If a part isn't exactly right? It gets the thumb!

The good doc is just as vehement about handling. No 4-4-2 (W-30 or otherwise) gets out of the laboratory without heavy-duty underpinnings—and stabilizer bars front *and* rear.

If you've been looking for the one that's got everything, now you know where to find it.

ENGINE

Type	W-30 Rocket V-8 (available)
Displacement, cubic inches	400
Bhp	360 at 5400 rpm
Torque, lb.-ft.	440 at 3600 rpm

Bore x stroke, inches	3.87 x 4.25
Compression ratio	10.5-to-1
Combustion chamber volume, min. allowable	79.64 cc
Min. deck clearance	0.002
Carburetion	Quadrajet 4-bbl.
Throttle dia.	
Primary	1.375
Secondary	2.250
Camshaft duration	
Intake	328°
Exhaust	328°
Overlap	108°
Total valve lift	
Intake	0.475
Exhaust	0.475

Valve diameter
Intake 2.0625
Exhaust 1.625
Tappet type .... Hydraulic
Max. valve spring pressure
Closed .... 128 lbs.
Crankshaft journal diameter
Mains 3.00
Connecting rods 2.50
Firing order 1-8-4-3-6-5-7-2
W-30 system includes 26.2-sq.-in. dual front air scoops; wide-throat dual air ducts; dual intake air cleaner; minimum combustion chamber volume; separated center exhaust ports for optimum tuning; streamlined, individually branched exhaust manifold; high-overlap cam; low-friction bearings; dual hood paint patches; and low-restriction dual exhausts.

Standard engines. A 400-cu.-in., 350-hp Rocket V-8 with heavy-duty 3-speed manual. A 400-cu.-in., 325-hp version with Turbo Hydra-matic 400.

DRIVE TRAIN

Transmission ...... Fully synchronized, heavy-duty 3-on-the-floor with Hurst Shifter. Available: 4-on-the-floor with close- or wide-ratio Hurst Shifter, or Turbo Hydra-matic 400. Special W-30 Turbo Hydra-matic 400 (with high-performance converter, high-rpm shift points, and firmed-up shifts) or close-ratio included with W-30.

8 axle ratios .... 2.56-to-1, 2.78-to-1, 3.08-to-1, 3.23-to-1, 3.42-to-1, 3.91-to-1, 4.33-to-1, 4.66-to-1. Availability depending on engine choice.

CHASSIS

Suspension .... Heavy-duty. Includes heavy-duty springs and shocks, front and rear stabilizers.

Steering ratio 24-to-1

Available: 17.5-to-1 with power.

Wheels ...... Heavy-duty 14-inch with 6-inch rims.

Tires ...... F70x14", polyester-cord wide-oval red-lines (or whitewalls). Available: F70x14" fiberglass-belted wide-oval red-line or wide-oval black-wall with raised white letters.

GENERAL

Models .. Holiday Coupe, Sports Coupe, Convertible

Wheelbase .... 112"

Overall length .... 201.9"

Curb wt. (lb.) Holiday Coupe ... 3675

Tread .... front 59.0", rear 59.0"

SAFETY

New GM safety features are standard, including seat belts for all passenger positions, and new ignition, steering and transmission lock on steering column.

A MATE FOR W-30.
WE LOOKED HARD.
BUT COULDN'T
FIND ONE.
SO THE GOOD
DOCTOR WENT BACK
TO WORK.
OLDS W-31.

Now meet the 1969 Mini-W. You'll know it better as W-31 — a 350-cuber with Force-Air Induction, increased hp rating, quick handling, great new styling, and an easy-going price that's bound to make it first choice in the mini-cube grab bag.

You can order yours in a gussied-up Cutlass S. Or you can play it straight and get it in a businesslike, minimum-weight F-85.

In any case, you get it with special behemoth hood paint patches.

And if you've a need to be personally involved, you've come to the right place. The good doc's list of available goodies is as long as your arm: 4 speeds with close- or wide-ratio, Anti-Spin Axle, tach, wide-boot blackwalls with raised white letters, Super Stock Wheels, and so on.

This year, have it *your* way.

ENGINE

Type	W-31 Rocket V-8 (available)
Displacement, cubic inches	350
Bhp	325 at 5400 rpm
Torque, lb.-ft.	360 at 3600 rpm
Bore x stroke, inches	4.057 x 3.385
Compression ratio	10.5-to-1
Combustion chamber volume, min. allowable	67.92 cc
Min. deck clearance	0.002
Carburetion	Quadrajet 4-bbl.
Throttle dia.	
Primary	1.375
Secondary	2.250
Camshaft duration	
Intake	308°
Exhaust	308°
Overlap	82°

2-bbl. carb, Rocket V-8. Available: 350-cu.-in., 310-hp, 4-bbl. carb version.

DRIVE TRAIN

Transmission . . . . . Fully synchronized, 3-speed manual. Heavy-duty floor-mounted Hurst Shifter version with W-31. Available: 4-on-the-floor with close- or wide-ratio Hurst Shifter.

8 axle ratios . . . . 2.56-to-1, 2.78-to-1, 3.08-to-1, 3.23-to-1, 3.42-to-1, 3.91-to-1, 4.33-to-1, 4.66-to-1. Availability depending on engine choice.

CHASSIS

Suspension . . Four-coil-spring with front stabilizer bar. Available: Heavy-duty shocks, front and rear.

Steering ratio 24-to-1
Available: 17.5-to-1 with power.

Wheels 14-inch
Available: 14"x6JK wheels.

Tires . . . . 7.75x14" blackwall
Available: 7.75x14" whitewalls; also wide-oval red-line or whitewall with

Total valve lift
Intake 0.474
Exhaust 0.474

Valve diameter
Intake 2.000
Exhaust 1.630

Tappet type . . . . Hydraulic

Crankshaft journal diameter
Mains 2.50
Connecting rods 2.125

Firing order 1-8-4-3-6-5-7-2

W-31 system includes 26.2-sq.-in. dual front air scoops; wide-throat dual air ducts; dual intake air cleaner; minimum combustion chamber volume; high-overlap cam; low-friction bearings; dual hood paint patches; and low-restriction dual exhausts.

Standard V-8 engine. 350-cu.-in., 250-hp,

polyester-cord or fiberglass-belting; plus new F70x14" wide-oval black-wall with raised white letters.

GENERAL

W-31 Models . . Available in Cutlass S and F-85 V-8 models.
Wheelbase . . . . .112"
Overall length . . . . 201.9"
Curb wt. (lb.) Holiday Coupe . . .3465
Tread . . . . front 59.0", rear 59.0"

SAFETY

New GM safety features are standard, including seat belts for all passenger positions, and new ignition, steering and transmission lock on steering column.

JUNIOR SUPER CARS

Junior Super Cars, such as the W-31 package, offer several advantages:

1. Easier to insure — Insurance companies set limitations on performance-car specifications for insurability — and the Junior Super Cars meet these limitations. Also, insurance companies recognize that these cars generally cost less to repair. Consequently, insurance is cheaper and easier to get.

2. Cost less initially — The F-85 coupe with the W-31 option costs $421.61 less than the W-30 4-4-2

W-30

The W-30 option is designed for "off-street" use. It is specifically engineered to use exhaust manifold leaders — an option **not** permitted on the street.

DMS 69–9&10

Dr. Oldsmobiles'
W Machines

W-30

AVAILABLE ON . . .

442 Sport Coupe

INCLUDES . . .

- 400 C.I.D. 360 H.P. engine with
  — high-performance distributor
  — special valve springs
  — Force-Air Induction
  — special matched and fitted components
- Dual stripe hood W-42
- W-30 front fender decals

MANDATORY OPTIONS . . .

- Anti-spin rear axle G-80
- Heavy-duty radiator V-01, V-02

OPTIONS NOT AVAILABLE . . .

- Air conditioning C-60
- Power brakes J50 or JL2
- Engine cooling equipment Y-72

TRANSMISSION AVAILABILITY . . .

- Four speed Hurst floor shifter
- Turbo Hydramatic

W-31

AVAILABLE ON . . .

F-85 Sport Coupe
Cutlass S Sport Coupe
Cutlass S Holiday Coupe
Cutlass S Convertible

INCLUDES . . .

- 350 C.I.D. 325 H.P. engine with
  — special quadrajet carburetor
  — Force-Air Induction
  — special valves
  — special camshaft
  — heavy-duty engine fan clutch
- W-31 front fender decals

MANDATORY OPTIONS . . .

- G-80 — Anti-spin rear axle
- V-01 — Heavy-duty radiator
- N-10 — Dual exhaust system

OPTIONS NOT AVAILABLE . . .

- C-60 — Air conditioning
- J50 or JL2 Power brakes (regular or disc)
- Y-72 — Engine cooling equipment

TRANSMISSION AVAILABILITY . . .

- Three speed Hurst floor shifter standard
- Four speed Hurst floor shifter wide ratio
- Four speed Hurst floor shifter close ratio
- Turbo Hydramatic

W-32

AVAILABLE ON . . .

442 Sport Coupe
442 Holiday Coupe
442 Convertible

INCLUDES . . .

- 400 C.I.D. 360 H.P. engine with
  — special camshaft
  — special distributor
  — heavy-duty water pump
  — aluminum fan and special fan clutch
- W-32 front fender decals

MANDATORY OPTIONS . . .

- Anti-spin rear axle G-80
- Heavy-duty radiator V-01, V-02
- Fiberglas belted tires P-81
- Special Turbo Hydramatic transmission M-YO
- Hood paint stripe Y-73

OPTIONS NOT AVAILABLE . . .

- A-93 Power door locks
- Y-72 Engine cooling equipment

Meet the muscle machine . . . the 1969 Hurst/Olds. It's a limited production custom special from Oldsmobile and Hurst Performance Research.

Now some people insist that the H/O on the hood scoop stands for hairy Olds . . . but we prefer to think it represents a bit more.

Here is the ultimate expression of Oldsmobile-engineered high-performance hardware . . . put together in a bold new custom package by Hurst.

And a potent package it is.

Up there in front sits a dual-inlet ozone grabber that appears as though it just might bite.

And it does. But only cold, dense, fresh air. It does it on demand, with vacuum-operated precision.

Then if you let your eye run rearward along the side and top you'll see those bold gold custom stripes.

And perched across the rear, sits the sexiest spoiler since Mata Hari. With its negative lift, it turns high-speed air turbulence into road-grabbing rear traction. Kind of a reverse-Wright-brothers effect.

Now we by-passed a few other outside goodies.

There are two dual low-drag racing-type outside mirrors . . . and distinctive Hurst/Olds emblems on the front quarter panels and rear deck lid.

That last one is going to get the most visibility.

And here's why.

That, sir, is the boss hoss of the Oldsmobile stable. All 455 cubic inches of it.

You get 500 pounds/feet of torque . . . which is enough to bend your mind, if nothing else.

It has special heads . . . a high-overlap cam . . . and a custom distributor advance curve tailored to do its thing at the right place and time.

Now all this muscle starts turning to hustle at the next stop.

A performance-modified Turbo Hydra-Matic that takes the twist and sends it out in silky squeals.

You can let the transmission do the talking . . . or you can take over and call the shot with the help of a slick Hurst Dual/Gate Shifter.

Either way it's music.

The rest of the path to the pavement is pure heavy duty.

Driveline, differential (3.42 to 1, anti-spin), axles, springs, shocks and a pair of husky anti-sway bars keep things nicely under control.

And oh yes.

Those big dual exhausts sing a song that is all their own.

One thing we can assure you.

With 455 cubes, a Hurst/Olds doesn't sing falsetto.

Now all is not go power.

The Hurst/Olds puts a stop to things with a pair of power front disc brakes that just refuse to blow their cool.

You get straight, sure stops everytime, with rapid heat dissipation and maximum fade resistance.

The stop and go departments are handled at the pavement by those fat, sticky Goodyear F60-15 Polyglas® tires.

And note what they ride on.

The rolling stock is comprised of special 7 inch Mag-Type steel wheels.

When they turn . . . so do the heads.

Inside, the Hurst/Olds also sports the custom touch.

Perched atop each handsome, pleated bucket seat is a custom gold-striped head restraint. It adds that regal touch to the interior . . . a bit of crowning glory if you'll pardon the expression.

And tucked down between the seats sits the Hurst Dual/Gate Shifter. It's the big stick that lets you choose your tone of voice at will. And it's sheer joy to slam that sturdy linkage up or down the gears. This is a shifter made to be shifted.

There is one more feature of the Hurst/Olds that we haven't mentioned.

Air Conditioning.

It's optional, of course, but there just isn't any way to beat the heat . . . or anything else . . . like an air conditioned Hurst/Olds.

It's almost like adding insult to injury.

1969 HURST/OLDS SPECIFICATIONS

GENERAL

Model	Modified 4-4-2 Holiday Coupe
Wheelbase	112.0
Length, overall	201.9
Width, overall	76.2
Height, overall	52.8
Track, front	61.0
Track, rear	60.0
Weight	3716 lbs.

ENGINE

Type	90° OHV V-8
Bore and Stroke	4.125 x 4.250
Displacement, cubic inches	455
Compression Ratio	10.5:1
Horsepower (@ rpm)	380 @ 5000
Torque (lb./ft. @ rpm)	500 @ 3200
Carburetor	4-bbl. Rochester 4 MV

ENGINE (Cont.)

Fuel	Premium
Air Induction	Special Cold Air w/ Hood Scoop
Intake Valve Duration	285°
Exhaust Valve Duration	287°
Valve Opening Overlap	57°
Valve Lift	0.472
Valve Lifters	Hydraulic
Exhaust System	Dual

TRANSMISSION (Std.)

Name	Turbo Hydra-Matic
Type	Modified 3-Speed Torque Converter
Gear Ratio, low	2.48
Gear Ratio, second	1.48
Gear Ratio, third	1.00
Gear Ratio, reverse	2.08
Torque Converter Ratio	2.30
Shift Mechanism	Hurst Dual/Gate

REAR AXLE

Type	Salisbury Live Hypoid, Semi Floating
Differential	Limited Slip, Multiple Plate Clutch
Axle Ratio (Std.)	3.42
Axle Ratio (Opt.)	3.91
Axle Ratio (A/C)	3.23

TIRES

Type and Manufacturer	Bias-Belted Goodyear Polyglas®
Size	F60 x 15

WHEELS

Type	Welded Steel
Size and Flange	15 x 7 JJ

BRAKES

Type	Power
Front	11 inch Disc
Rear	9.5 inch Drum

All dimensions are in inches unless otherwise indicated.

While the information herein was in effect when approved for printing, Hurst Performance Research Inc. reserves the right to change specifications, design or prices without notice and without liability therefor.

Looking at the 85 years Oldsmobile has been vending its automotive products, 1970 stands as the ultimate year for the high performance cars from Lansing. The 4-4-2 series continued to offer good basic levels of balanced automotive performance, particularly when dollars spent were examined. In addition, there were the W-cars, the single-year offering of the Rallye 350. With the help of strong sales of its performance cars, Olds hung onto a fifth place standing in the industry with 633,981 sales.

In 1970, a 4-4-2 convertible paced America's most famous auto race—the Indianapolis 500, the first time in a decade Oldsmobile had been so honored. The pearl white 4-4-2s were fitted with white tops, black interiors and red stripes. Some replicas were sold at Olds dealerships and the actual pace car was awarded to race winner Al Unser.

The standard powerplant this year on the 4-4-2 was the 365 hp, 455 cid V-8. Olds called its 4-4-2 suspension the Rally-Sports system and it consisted of heavy-duty springs (front and rear), shocks, stabilizer bars and rear suspension lower control arms. The package also included a heavy-duty driveshaft, motor mounts and seven inch wide rims fitted with G-70x14 whitewall wide-oval tires.

Again, three versions were available in the 4-4-2 series. Rarest of the trio was the sport coupe, model 4477. It was priced at $3,312 and just 1,688 were built. This was the last year for the pillared coupe as a 4-4-2. The 4-4-2 convertible was designated model 4467. Production—including pace car replicas—was 2,933, with prices beginning at $3,567. The overwhelming favorite in the Olds performance series was model number 4487—the hardtop coupe. Production was 14,709, and prices began at $3,376.

This year Olds numbered most of its performance options with a "W" prefix. W-25 was the $157 dual intake fiberglass hood; W-26 was the $76 console with Hurst Dual Gate shifter; W-27 was the $57 aluminum rear axle carrier and cover, and W-35 was the $73 rear decklid spoiler.

The W-cars were alive and well in 1970. The W-30 again was in the 4-4-2 section of the dealer order book. The package cost $369 and at the heart of it was a 370 hp Rocket V-8. It was fed by forced air induction and had a special air cleaner, aluminum intake manifold, special body stripes, sports mirrors and a lightweight body insulation package. The W-32 was a special performance package for the Cutlass Supreme series. It used a 365 hp, 455 cid V-8 and cost $141. The potent W-31 was still available this year and cost $368. It consisted of a forced air induction 325 hp, 350 cid small block engine with aluminum intake manifold, heavy-duty clutch, disc brakes, special hood and paint stripes and external W-31 emblems. This package could be ordered on selected Cutlass S and F-85 models.

The new kid on the Oldsmobile performance block in 1970 was the Rallye 350—option W-45. This was a single-year Olds offering and it was available in just a single color—bright Sebring Yellow. An orange and black decal package was part of the Rallye 350 package along with urethane coated front and rear yellow bumpers, yellow Super Stock II wheels, G-70x14 wide oval tires and a 350 cid small block powerplant.

Olds probably produced more literature this year dedicated to high performance than any other year before or since. There was a nifty catalogue devoted strictly to the W-cars and performance options for 1970. It replaced the previous 1969 black-and-white format with nice four-color printing (see pages 69-80).* Oldsmobile's ad agency billed its new products as "Escape Machines" and the four-color full-line catalogue carried that theme. The 4-4-2 rated four pages in that full-line piece and there was an additional page on the W-cars (see pages 64-68).* The Rallye 350 had a pair of specially printed pieces—a color folder (see pages 81-84)* and a small black-and-white brochure designed mainly for the Olds dealer sales force (see pages 85-96).*

*Front covers shown below.

4-4-2.

Ask the man who knows one.

Over the past few years 4-4-2 has won more accolades, trophies, and believers than you can shake a 4-speed at. Oh, don't get us wrong. The competition is tough. And doing a great job—in some places.

Some offer outstanding performance, but look like boxcars. Others are real eye-poppers, but ride (ouch!) like buckboards.

Olds figures if you *really* like cars, you should be able to get your driving gloves on a machine that's got it all.

Have at it—4-4-2 for 1970!

Under the 4-4-2 hood rumbles *as large a V-8 as has ever been bolted into a special-performance production automobile! 455 cubic inches! And it's standard!*

Want the head-turning look of a special fiberglass hood with dual air-scoops, big rally stripes, locking hood pins, plus cold-air induction? Then order the new W-25 performance / appearance package — and you've got it!

Either way, underpinnings are heavy-duty, as you'd expect. But then we go one step further with stabilizer bars both *front and rear.* Also standard. So you ride with unexpected and unequaled smoothness— and downright fantastic handling. On the straightaway or through the esses! (Watch for the imitators to copy this one.)

As for looks? Be our guest.

And the sound? Like music—through low-restriction dual exhausts. "The way it is" is good enough for others. But only "the way it *ought* to be" is good enough for the 1970 4-4-2. And you.

Long days. Lonely nights. How the hours drag. Wouldn't it be nice to have an Escape Machine?

4-4-2 Holiday Coupe.

14

Olds offers, at modest extra cost, a variety of options and accessories, many of which are shown in the car illustrations, and are also described on pages 44, 46, and 47.

4-4-2's best-of-everything attitude isn't limited to performance and handling, as you can plainly see. This is the Strato Bucket Seat interior of the 4-4-2 Convertible—a rugged and handsome combination Walrus-Grain Morocceen with Madrid Morocceen accents. The completely new sports console, power windows, and Deluxe Seat Belts are available as shown.

Olds offers, at modest extra cost, a variety of options and accessories, many of which are shown in the car illustrations, and are also described on pages 44, 46, and 47.

4-4-2 Sports Coupe

4-4-2 Convertible

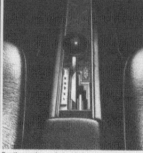

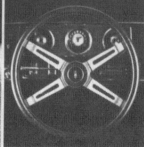

Handsome, louvered 7" Super Stock Wheels and big, black, bias-ply, glass-belted tires with raised white letters, available. Heavy-duty 7" wheels and white-stripe wide-ovals, standard.

For those who can't decide between a manual or an automatic—there's our new Dual-Gate Shifter. It gives you the best of both. Order it for your console.

Special 4-spoke brushed-metal Custom-Sport Steering Wheel, available. Features a special soft leather-grain-vinyl rim for positive non-slip grip. Rocket Rally Pac, available.

17

Olds offers, at modest extra cost, a variety of options and accessories, many of which are shown in the car illustrations, and are also described on pages 44, 46, and 47.

The 1970 W-Machines: W-30 and W-31. Special packages for special application!

Cutlass S W-31   4-4-2 W-30 in special new Rally Red

With the W-Machines you get extra horsepower out of thin air! Their specially designed fiber-glass hood scoops grab cold air and ram it into the wide-throat Quadrajet carb. And that's where the magic happens! The quick-moving cold air mixes with vaporized gasoline. A super-dense air/fuel mixture results. And so does extra usable horsepower!

W-30 PACKAGE: Available in 4-4-2 Coupes, Convertible. Includes fiberglass hood with cold-air hood scoops; dual hood pin locks; big rally stripes on hood, plus side-body stripes; two sport-styled outside mirrors (left-hand mirror with remote control); die-cast "W"

identification on front fenders; special 455-cube, cold-air V-8 with "select fit" of critical parts; performance-calibrated 4-bbl cold-air carburetor; low-restriction air cleaner; light-weight aluminum manifold; high-overlap cam; manual disc brakes up front, large drums in back; heavy-duty radiator and power-saving clutch fan; reduced body sound deadener; super-wide G70 x 14" bias-ply, glass-belted blackwalls with raised white letters mounted on heavy-duty 7-inch wheels; Anti-Spin axle. Not included in the W-30 package, but already standard in 4-4-2 are full dual exhausts and heavy-duty FE2 suspension

with front and rear stabilizer bars.

W-31 PACKAGE: Available in Cutlass S and F-85 Coupes only. It includes all equipment listed for W-30, with the following exception: In place of the 455-cubic-inch V-8, a special 350-cubic-inch cold-air V-8 with "select fit" of critical parts is featured.

A few additional goodies you may wish to order: Special new Rally Red or Sebring Yellow exterior paint. Close- or wide-ratio 4-speed. Performance-calibrated Turbo Hydra-matic. New Dual-Gate Automatic.

See your Olds dealer for a more complete list of special 1970 W-Machine equipment.

18

DR. OLDSMOBILE'S 4-4-2 AND W-MACHINES
Detailed 4-4-2, W-30, and W-31 specifications; special packages; new performance parts and accessories; plus an order form inside.

FOR 1970, DR. OLDSMOBILE INTRODUCES AS LARGE A V-8 AS EVER BOLTED INTO A SPECIAL-PERFORMANCE PRODUCTION AUTOMOBILE!

There's more than one way to make a car run.

You can load up on cubic inches. Or you can cut down on excess weight.

For 1970, the good doctor accomplished both.

He's come up with a new 455-cube V-8 that actually weighs in lighter than last year's 400-cube job!

It's big. It's strong. And it's standard —in every 1970 Olds 4-4-2!

Here's how a 455-powered 4-4-2 dresses out when ordered with the good W-Machine equipment . . .

4-4-2 W-MACHINE SPECS

Engine type	H.C. air-inducted W-30 Rocket V-8
Displacement	455 cu. in.
Bhp	370 at 5200 rpm
Torque, lb.-ft.	500 at 3600 rpm
Bore x stroke, in.	4.125 x 4.250
Compression ratio	10.50-to-1
Combustion chamber volume, min. allowable	91.72 cc
Min. cyl. head vol.	69.75 cc
Min. deck clearance	.002 below
Carburetion	Quadrajet 4-bbl performance-calibrated

4-4-2 W-30

Olds offers, at modest extra cost, a variety of options and accessories, many of which are shown in the car illustrations.

Intake manifold ....Aluminum
Camshaft duration
  Intake, exhaust ....328°
Camshaft overlap
  Intake, exhaust ....108°
Total valve lift
  Intake, exhaust 475
Valve diameter (Max.)
  Intake 2.077
  Exhaust 1.630
Brakes ....Manual discs, front.
  9.5-inch drums, rear
Transmission .... Full sync h-d close-
  ratio 4-speed with Hurst Competi-

tion Shifter, or beefed, performance-
calibrated Turbo Hydra-matic 400,
required.
Axle ....3.42 Anti-Spin
Exhaust system ....Full duals
Cooling system ....H-d radiator
  and power-saving clutch fan
Suspension FE2
  Includes h-d springs, shocks, control
  arms, plus stabilizer bars front and
  rear.
Wheels ....H-d 14" with 7" rim
Tires PK5
  G70 x 14" bias-ply, glass-belted

blackwalls with raised white letters.
Mirrors ....Two sports-styled
  outside mirrors (left-side with remote control).
Also included in W-30: Lightweight
fiberglass hood with functional scoops,
big hood stripes, chromed hood tie-
downs, and low-restriction air cleaner
(W25). "Select fit" engine parts.
Reduced body sound deadener. Special paint stripes along body sides.
Die-cast W-30 identification on front
fenders. Strato Bucket Seats are standard in all 4-4-2 models.

THE GOOD DOC GOT BUSY INSIDE TOO. MEET THE FIRST HEAVY-DUTY SHIFTER MOUNTED IN BUTTER!

Bolt a stick onto a really tough 3- or 4-speed gear-box and you've got a back-busting shifting job ahead of you, right? Wrong!

The good Doc has that problem completely trailered.

He's coupled beefed, precision gearing with that irrepressible Hurst Competition Shifter.

Fast? Easy? You go through the digits like a hot knife whips through butter! Here's how Olds Cutlass S (or F-85) stacks up when ordered with complete W-Machine equipment . . .

CUTLASS S W-MACHINE SPECS

Engine type	H.C. air-inducted W-31 Rocket V-8
Displacement	350 cu. in.
Bhp	325 at 5400 rpm
Torque, lb.-ft.	360 at 3600 rpm
Bore x stroke, in.	4.057 x 3.385
Compression ratio	10.50-to-1
Combustion chamber volume, min. allowable	67.92 cc
Min. cyl. head vol.	60.58 cc
Min. deck clearance	.002 below
Carburetion	Quadrajet 4-bbl performance-calibrated

CUTLASS S W-31

Intake manifold . . . . Aluminum
Camshaft duration
  Intake, exhaust . . . . .308°
Camshaft overlap
  Intake, exhaust . . . . .82°
Total valve lift
  Intake .474
  Exhaust 474
Valve diameter (Max.)
  Intake 2.005
  Exhaust 1.630
Brakes . . . . Manual discs, front.
  9.5-inch drums, rear
Transmission . . . Full sync h-d 3-on-the-

floor with Hurst Competition Shifter;
close- or wide-ratio h-d 4-speed
with Hurst Competition Shifter; or
beefed, performance-calibrated
Turbo Hydra-matic 350, required.
Axle . . . . 3.91 Anti-Spin
Cooling system . . . Extra h-d radiator
  and power-saving clutch fan
Suspension FE2
  Includes h-d springs, shocks, control
  arms, plus stabilizer bars front and
  rear.
Wheels . . . . H-d 14" with 7" rim
Tires PK5

G70 x 14" bias-ply, glass-belted
  blackwalls with raised white letters.
Mirrors . . . . Two sports-styled
  outside mirrors (left-side with remote control).
Exhaust system . . . . Full duals
Also included in W-31: Lightweight
fiberglass hood with functional scoops,
big hood stripes, chromed hood tie-
downs, and low-restriction air cleaner
(W25). "Select fit" engine parts. Reduced body sound deadener. Special
paint stripes along body sides. Die-cast
W-31 identification on front fenders.

Olds offers, at modest extra cost, a variety of options and accessories, many of which are shown in the car illustrations.

DR. O EMERGES FROM THE WIND TUNNEL. AND A COMPETITION-CHILLING, UNDER-HOOD BLIZZARD IS BORN!

There are all kinds of hood scoops around. Many of them are just for looks. And a lot of others might just as well be.

Dr. Oldsmobile figures if you're going to do something, you ought to do it up big.

That means designing and testing air-grabbing scoops that are big enough and placed forward far enough to really do the job.

Cold-Air Induction will never replace cubes or high-compression (which Olds already has plenty of). But Cold-Air can be icing on the cake by getting you extra hp out of thin air—when done properly!

OLDS 4-4-2 SPECS

Engine type	H.C. Rocket V-8
Displacement	455 cu. in.
Bhp	365 at 5000 rpm
Torque, lb.-ft.	500 at 3200 rpm
Bore x stroke, in.	4.125 x 4.250
Compression ratio	10.50-to-1
Combustion chamber volume, min. allowable	91.72 cc
Min. cyl. head vol.	69.75 cc
Min. deck clearance	.002 below
Carburetion	Quadrajet 4-bbl
Camshaft duration	
Intake/exhaust (Sync)	294 /296
Intake/exhaust (Auto)	285 /287
Camshaft overlap	
Intake/exhaust (Sync)	68
Intake/exhaust (Auto)	57
Total valve lift	
Intake/exhaust	.472
Valve diameter (Max.)	
Intake	2.077
Exhaust	1.630
Brakes	9.5" drums, 157.8 sq. in. lining area
Transmission	Full sync h-d 3-on-the-floor with Hurst Competition Shifter.
Axle (Sync)	3.08 ratio
Exhaust system	Full duals
Suspension	FE2

Includes h-d springs, shock, control arms, plus stabilizer bars front and rear.

Wheels	H-d 14" with 7" rim
Tires	P26

G70 bias-ply, glass-belted with white stripe.

Strato Bucket Seats, standard in all 4-4-2 models.

Lightweight fiberglass hood, functional scoops, big hood stripes, chromed hood tie-downs, and low-restriction air cleaner (W25), available.

NOSE AROUND IN THE GOOD DOC'S PARTS BIN AND HERE'S JUST A FEW THINGS YOU'RE LIKELY TO FIND...

M21 Heavy-Duty Close-Ratio 4-Speed. Fully synchronized. Features helical-cut forged gears, forged gearshafts, high-capacity bearings, lightweight aluminum case, and Hurst Competition Shifter. Ratios: 2.20:1, 1.64:1, 1.28:1, 1.00:1, 2.60:1 (reverse). Required with manual W-30.

M20 Heavy-Duty Wide-Ratio 4-Speed (with same features as M21). Ratios: 2.52:1, 1.88:1, 1.46:1, 1.00:1, 2.60:1 (reverse). Not available in 4-4-2 models.

M40 Beefed Turbo Hydra-matic 400. Performance-calibrated. 3-speeds forward. Features high-performance torque converter, high rpm shift points, and firmed-up shifts. Available in W-30 only. 350 version (M38) available in W-31 only.

D35 Sports-Styled Outside Mirrors. Aerodynamically designed for low wind resistance. Color-keyed to body color. Left-side mirror features remote control.

N34 Custom-Sport Steering Wheel. Has four brushed-metal spokes and soft, leather-grain-vinyl rim for positive, non-slip grip.

PK5 Super-Wide G70 x 14″ Tires. Bias-ply, glass-belted blackwalls with raised white letters. They really put a foot down.

U21 Rocket Rally Pac. Includes 7000-rpm dash-mounted tach, clock, plus temperature and oil pressure gauges.

W25 Hood. New Performance/Appearance Package for 1970. Available on all 4-4-2 and Cutlass S 4-bbl models.

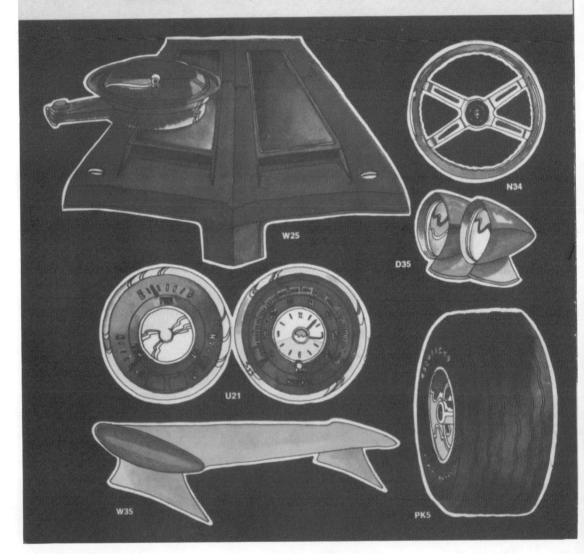

W25 · N34 · D35 · U21 · W35 · PK5

Included in W-30, W-31 packages. Features lightweight fiberglass hood with functional air scoops, chromed hood tie-downs, big hood stripes, and low-restriction air cleaner.

W26 Hurst Dual-Gate Shifter in Sports Console. For those who are torn between a manual or automatic. This one gives you a handful of both. Available with bucket seat models only. Features Hurst Shifter and lighted, lockable map compartment.

W27 Aluminum Axle Carrier and Cover. Reduces weight over the conventional cast iron carrier by more than 22 pounds. Available with W-30, W-31, and W-32 only.

FE2 Special Heavy-Duty Suspension. Includes heavy-duty springs, shocks,

and lower control arms, plus stabilizer bars both *front and rear!* The imitators are already popping up faster than you can say "me too."

W35 New Rear-Deck Spoiler. Full-width fiberglass wing with up-swept tips. Color-keyed to body color. Designed for increased rear-wheel traction at higher speeds.

P05 Super Stock I Wheels—bold and beefy. N66 Super Stock II Wheels—with big, see-through louvers. N95 For that wire-wheel look.

SPECIAL NOTE: Three new performance packages now available, including two for full-size 1970 Olds models. W32 Cutlass Supreme Performance Package. Available with Cutlass Su-

preme SX package only. Features a Quadrajet 4-bbl carburetor; along with the 455-cube, high-compression V-8, Turbo Hydra-matic 400 transmission, dual exhausts, and distinctive ornamentation which are included in the SX package.

W33 Olds 88 Performance Package. Available in all Delta 88 models with automatic transmission. Package includes a high-performance 455-cube/390-hp Rocket V-8, 4-bbl carb, dual exhausts, and 2.93-to-1 axle.

W34 Toronado GT Package. Includes high-performance 455-cube/400-hp Rocket V-8, 4-bbl carb, dual exhausts, special performance-calibrated Turbo Hydra-matic 400 transmission, "GT" hood emblem, custom paint striping.

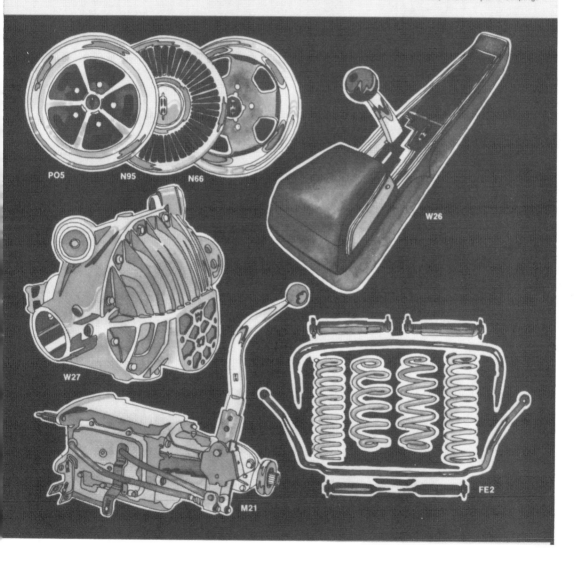

PO5 N95 N66 W26 W27 M21 FE2

GETTING YOUR 4-4-2 OR W-MACHINE
EXACTLY THE WAY YOU WANT IT!

(To expedite matters, simply check the boxes below which indicate the equipment and level of performance you're after.

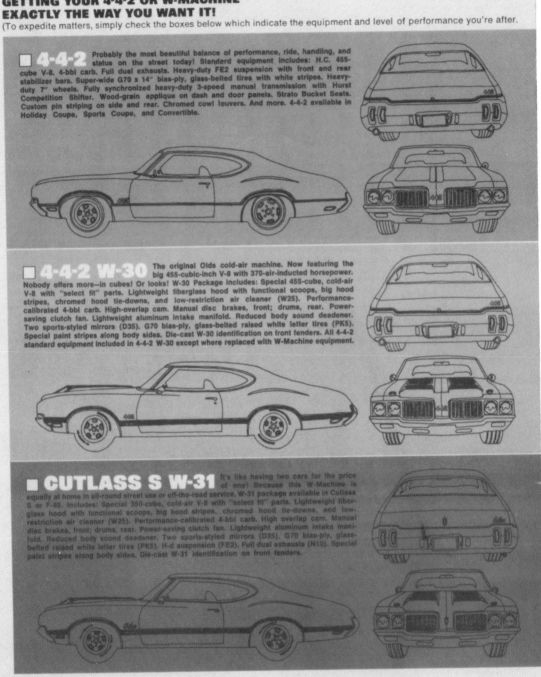

☐ **4-4-2** Probably the most beautiful balance of performance, ride, handling, and status on the street today! Standard equipment includes: H.C. 455-cube V-8, 4-bbl carb. Full dual exhausts. Heavy-duty FE2 suspension with front and rear stabilizer bars. Super-wide G70 x 14" bias-ply, glass-belted tires with white stripes. Heavy-duty 7" wheels. Fully synchronized heavy-duty 3-speed manual transmission with Hurst Competition Shifter. Wood-grain applique on dash and door panels. Strato Bucket Seats. Custom pin striping on side and rear. Chromed cowl louvers. And more. 4-4-2 available in Holiday Coupe, Sports Coupe, and Convertible.

☐ **4-4-2 W-30** The original Olds cold-air machine. Now featuring the big 455-cubic-inch V-8 with 370-air-inducted horsepower. Nobody offers more—in cubes! Or looks! W-30 Package includes: Special 455-cube, cold-air V-8 with "select fit" parts. Lightweight fiberglass hood with functional scoops, big hood stripes, chromed hood tie-downs, and low-restriction air cleaner (W25). Performance-calibrated 4-bbl carb. High-overlap cam. Manual disc brakes, front; drums, rear. Power-saving clutch fan. Lightweight aluminum intake manifold. Reduced body sound deadener. Two sports-styled mirrors (D35). G70 bias-ply, glass-belted raised white letter tires (PK5). Special paint stripes along body sides. Die-cast W-30 identification on front fenders. All 4-4-2 standard equipment included in 4-4-2 W-30 except where replaced with W-Machine equipment.

☐ **CUTLASS S W-31** It's like having two cars for the price of one! Because this W-Machine is equally at home in all-round street use or off-the-road service. W-31 package available in Cutlass S or F-85. Includes: Special 350-cube, cold-air V-8 with "select fit" parts. Lightweight fiberglass hood with functional scoops, big hood stripes, chromed hood tie-downs, and low-restriction air cleaner (W25). Performance-calibrated 4-bbl carb. High overlap cam. Manual disc brakes, front; drums, rear. Power-saving clutch fan. Lightweight aluminum intake manifold. Reduced body sound deadener. Two sports-styled mirrors (D35). G70 bias-ply, glass-belted raised white letter tires (PK5). H-d suspension (FE2). Full dual exhausts (N10). Special paint stripes along body sides. Die-cast W-31 identification on front fenders.

Then get with your Olds dealer.)

Available with 4-4-2:

☐ **W25 Lightweight fiberglass hood** with functional scoops, big hood stripes, chromed hood tie-downs, and low-restriction air cleaner (Included in W-30).

☐ **W26 Dual-Gate Shifter in Console.** Includes Hurst Shifter, console, wood-grain applique, lockable (and lighted) map compartment, front and rear console lamps. M40 required.

☐ **D55 Sports Console.** Includes transmission shift lever, wood-grain applique, and lockable map compartment.

☐ **W-30** See listing of W-30 package components under 4-4-2 W-30 on facing page.

☐ **D35 Two sports-styled outside mirrors** (left-side with remote control).

☐ **G80 Anti-Spin Performance Axle.** Automatically shifts power to wheel with best traction. Included in G88, G92.

☐ **G88 Performance Axle Package.** 3.91-to-1. Includes extra-heavy-duty radiator and power-saving clutch fan, Anti-Spin, and heavy-duty axle shafts.

☐ **G92 Performance Axle Package.** 3.42-to-1. Includes heavy-duty radiator, Anti-Spin, and heavy-duty axle shafts.

☐ **4.33-, 4.66-, 5.00-to-1 axle ratios** also available, dealer installed. (Not recommended for street use.)

☐ **M21 Fully synchronized, heavy-duty, close-ratio 4-speed transmission.** Includes Hurst Competition Shifter and 3.42 axle ratio.

☐ **M40 Turbo Hydra-matic 400 automatic.** Three forward speeds. Includes 3.23 axle ratio.

☐ **N34 Custom-Sport Steering Wheel.** 4-spoke, with soft leather-grain-vinyl non-slip rim.

☐ **N47 Vari-Ratio Power Steering.**

☐ **JL2 Power Brakes** with discs up front.

☐ **N66 Super Stock II Wheels.**

☐ **N95 Simulated Wire Wheels.**

☐ **P05 Super Stock I Wheels.**

☐ **U21 Rocket Rally Pac.** Includes 7000-rpm tach, clock, plus temperature and oil gauges.

☐ **W35 Rear-Deck Spoiler,** fiberglass.

☐ **Y73 GT Hood Paint Stripes.** Not available with W-25 or W-30.

To assure the ultimate in performance and reliability, the following items are required when ordering your 4-4-2 W-Machine:

☐ **M21 Fully synchronized, heavy-duty close-ratio 4-speed transmission.** Includes Hurst Competition Shifter.
OR

☐ **M40 Special "W" Turbo Hydra-matic 400.** Includes high-performance torque converter, high rpm shift points, and firmed-up shifts.

☐ **G91 Axle, 3.23-to-1.** With C60.

☐ **G92 Performance Axle Package.** 3.42-to-1. Includes heavy-duty radiator, Anti-Spin, and heavy-duty axle shafts.

Available with 4-4-2 W-30:

☐ **C60 Air Conditioning.** Now available on W-30 with 3.23-to-1 axle ratio. M40 and JL2 required.

☐ **W27 Aluminum Axle Carrier and Cover.**

☐ **W26 Dual-Gate Shifter in Console.** Includes Hurst Shifter, console, wood-grain applique, lockable (and lighted) map compartment, front and rear console lamps. M40 required.

☐ **D55 Sports Console** with transmission shift lever. Includes wood-grain applique and lockable map compartment.

☐ **G88 Performance Axle Package.** 3.91-to-1. Includes extra-heavy-duty radiator, Anti-Spin, and heavy-duty axle shafts. Recommended for off-highway use.

☐ **4.33-, 4.66-, and 5.00-to-1 ratios available**—dealer installed. (Not recommended for street use.)

☐ **N34 Custom-Sport Steering Wheel.** 4-spoke, with soft leather-grain-vinyl non-slip rim.

☐ **N47 Vari-Ratio Power Steering.**

☐ **JL2 Power Brakes** with discs up front (automatic only).

☐ **N66 Super Stock II Wheels.**

☐ **N95 Simulated Wire Wheels.**

☐ **P05 Super Stock I Wheels.**

☐ **U21 Rocket Rally Pac.** Includes 7000-rpm tach, clock, plus temperature and oil gauges.

☐ **W35 Rear-Deck Spoiler,** fiberglass.

To assure the ultimate in performance and reliability, the following items are required when ordering your F-85 or Cutlass S W-Machine:

☐ **M14 Fully synchronized, heavy-duty 3-speed manual transmission.** Includes Hurst Competition Shifter.
OR

☐ **M20 Fully synchronized, heavy-duty wide-ratio 4-speed manual transmission.** Includes Hurst Competition Shifter.
OR

☐ **M21 Fully synchronized, heavy-duty close-ratio 4-speed manual transmission.** Includes Hurst Competition Shifter.
OR

☐ **M36 Special "W" Turbo Hydra-matic 350.** Includes high-performance torque converter, high rpm shift points, and firmed-up shifts.

☐ **G88 Performance Axle Package.** 3.91-to-1. Includes extra-heavy-duty radiator, Anti-Spin, and heavy-duty axle shafts.
OR

☐ **G92 Performance Axle Package.** 3.42-to-1. Includes heavy-duty radiator, Anti-Spin, and heavy-duty axle shafts.

Available with W-31:

☐ **W27 Aluminum Axle Carrier and Cover.**

☐ **W26 Dual-Gate Shifter in Console.** Includes Hurst Shifter, console, wood-grain applique, lockable (and lighted) map compartment, front and rear console lamps. M40 required.

☐ **D55 Sports Console** with transmission shift lever. Includes wood-grain applique and lockable map compartment.

☐ **4.33-, 4.66-, and 5.00-to-1 ratios available**—dealer installed. (Not recommended for street use.)

☐ **N34 Custom-Sport Steering Wheel.** 4-spoke, with soft leather-grain-vinyl non-slip rim.

☐ **N47 Vari-Ratio Power Steering.**

☐ **N66 Super Stock II Wheels.**

☐ **N95 Simulated Wire Wheels.**

☐ **P05 Super Stock I Wheels.**

☐ **U21 Rocket Rally Pac.** Includes 7000-rpm tach, clock, plus temperature and oil gauges.

☐ **W35 Rear-Deck Spoiler,** fiberglass.

For comfort and convenience accessories available with 4-4-2, W-30, and W-31, see your Olds dealer.

Olds offers, at modest extra cost, a variety of options and accessories, many of which are shown in the car illustrations.

Oldsmobile Introduces . . .
RALLYE 350
The New Action Look

a. Sebring Yellow body color; urethane-coated bumpers in matching color; blacked-out grille sections. **b.** Special Super Stock Wheels (yellow spider & rim). **c.** Air-inducted Rocket 350 V-8 H.C., 4-Bbl. Engine. **d.** Rear-Deck Air Spoiler", bold black and orange body decals accentuate the hood, front fender and rear body silhouette line. **e.** Custom-Sport Steering Wheel with grained vinyl, non-slip grip. Other features include: • Dual sports-styled, outside rearview mirrors • Dual-intake, Force-Air fiberglass hood with chromed hood latches • Special FE2 Suspension with front and rear stabilizer bars • Special notched rear bumper with flared dual exhausts • G70 x 14" bias-belted wide-oval blackwall tires • 3.23:1 standard axle.

"One of the many available options for your Rallye 350.

ACTION-LOOK RALLYE 350 . . . EASY TO BUY, EASY TO DRIVE!

New head-turning styling—Distinctive Sebring Yellow body paint with blacked-out grille. Special sports stripes (hood, sides and rear). Functional hood scoops. Sports mirrors. Special Super Stock Wheels. And more! A bold new look that'll turn the head of even the most sophisticated neighbor.

Surefooted ride and handling—A 310-hp Rocket 350 V-8 with 4-barrel carburetor provides the performance. And a special FE2 Suspension with front and rear stabilizer bars provides a ride and handling that's tough to beat. In the straightaway. Or when cornering. Super-wide, bias-belted blackwalls mounted on special 7-inch Super Stock Wheels give you great traction and add to the action look. Olds Rallye 350 is meant to be driven.

Special urethane-coated bumpers that match the body color —A great styling innovation! And highly practical, too. Factory tests show that these handsome coated bumpers offer exceptional resistance to both chipping and corrosion. So, they'll stay handsome for a long, long time. The rear bumper, incidentally, is specially notched for flared dual exhaust outlets.

Surprisingly low price — Truly a budget-pleasing all-action car. The Rallye 350 offers you the look, the feel, the drive and performance you want . . . all at a price that will prove you're closer to Oldsmobile than you think! A wide range of available equipment is offered to make your Rallye 350 distinctively yours. Come in. Test drive one and be ready to go Olds!

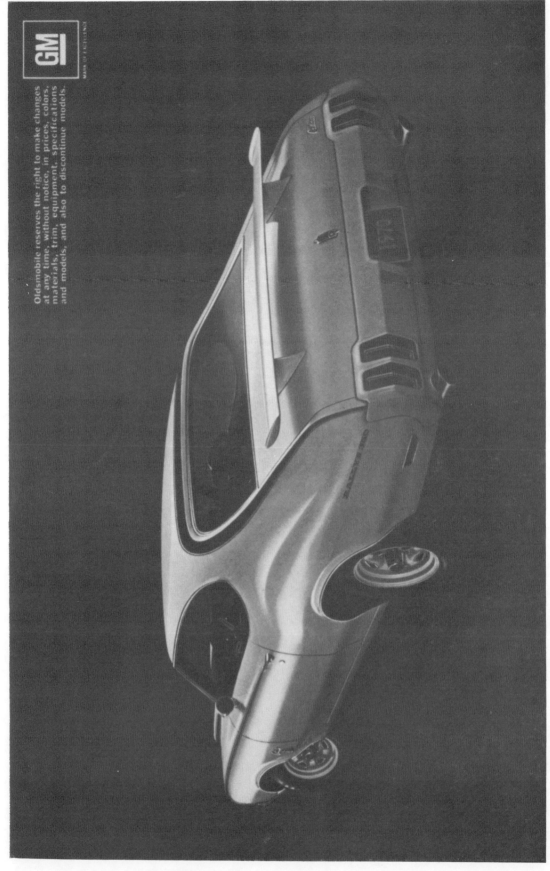

RALLYE '350

OLDSMOBILE'S CHALLENGE TO 1970's MID-YEAR INTERMEDIATE COMPETITION...

A SPECIAL MESSAGE TO
OLDSMOBILE SALESMEN.

New sales opportunities await you with the introduction of Oldsmobile's RALLYE 350...

... a car with high visibility priced to more than hold its own in the intermediate segment of the market.

Here's a car loaded with selling features, but two stand out crystal-clear. It's priced right for those prospects who wish to be identified with the look of performance. Yet its more practical engine and power train could well result in substantial savings in insurance. Ponder that in this market of rising costs.

Rallye 350 is offered in three V-8 models . . . Cutlass S Hardtop Coupe, Cutlass S Sports Coupe, and the F-85 Coupe, all with black interior trim.

Your option number for ordering the Rallye 350 Appearance Package is W45 which includes:

- Sebring Yellow Paint
- Black and Orange Body Decals for the Hood, Front Fender Peaks and Rear Body Silhouette Peak Line
- Rallye 350 Decal on the Rear Fender Over-hang
- Blacked-Out Grille
- Painted (yellow) Super Stock II Wheels
- 670 x 14" Bias Belted Wide Oval Blackwall Tires
- Urethane-coated Front and Rear Bumpers in Matching Body Color

Manufacturers Suggested Retail Price $157.98

THE MARKET

The Rallye 350 fits competitively into an existing product group made up of performance appearance packages added to intermediate price leader models. Competitive makes are the Plymouth Road Runner, Ford Torino with the GT option and Dodge Super Bee.

Pontiac's GTO Judge is similar in appearance. But the "Judges" are top-of-the-line intermediates with a much higher price tag and a standard ultra-high performance engine and power train.

Our Rallye 350 is offered with the L74 (Cutlass Supreme) engine. It provides unquestioned performance at a level that may offer substantial insurance rate benefits to the buyer.

Remember this . . . the Rallye 350 will find its greatest appeal to the prospect who wishes to identify with the "performance look" . . . the NOW look . . . that has been happily combined with the practical aspects of a more conventional engine and power train.

In substance, it's for the intermediate "doll package" prospect who is keenly aware of competition and their prices. There's no doubt about it . . . this type of product concept as represented by the Rallye 350 has gained a high degree of consumer acceptance on the strength of unusual appearance, relatively low price, and practicality.

INSURANCE

As previously stated, a key feature in selling the Rallye 350 is "insurability". The more practical horsepower rating of the Rallye 350 could obviously translate itself into insurance benefits. Insurance rates vary by locality. It would be wise to check your local rates or visit with insurance representatives to learn just what these benefits would be.

But let's dwell on the W45 Appearance Package once more. Make no mistake, it is exceptionally priced at $157.98. If these items were available as separate options, an approximate dollar value of more than $210.00 would be assigned at Manufacturer's Suggested Retail.

In addition to the above, the Rallye 350 (Option W45) also requires the following additional items:

W25 Force-Air Fiberglass Hood

L74 350 cu. in. 350 h.p. high compression engine with standard 3/23:1 axle ratio

N10 Dual Exhaust System

FE2 Rallye-Sport Suspension with front and rear stabilizer bars

D35 Sports-styled Outside Mirrors

N34 Custom-Sport Steering Wheel

A basic 3277 F-85 Sports Coupe equipped with the Rallye 350 option and six required items has a manufacturer's suggested retail price of $3252.84. It is actually $67.16 less than a comparably equipped Plymouth Road Runner ($3,320.00).

A real red-hot selling feature is the urethane-coated bumper material of the Rallye 350. This is a magic-like substance that can be likened to an "elastic plastic". It is applied to the metal bumper forming a protective coat of urethane in yellow primer color. Baked out at 250 degrees Farenheit the bumper is then sprayed with Sebring Yellow paint. A urethane (pronounced you-ra-thane) coated surface has a number of advantages over both painted and chrome plated bumper surfaces. Exhaustive tests have proved its superior resistance to minor abrasions, corrosion, blisters, chipping, and has also shown a marked indifference to an assortment of scratches and scars. As for minor dents, the urethane treated bumper can be "banged out" without having to refinish the surface.

When subjected to more severe dents, the surface can be restored to its off-the-line condition by sanding and repainting it with a urethane lacquer. Other tests have proved without question that urethane coated bumpers are superior to paint and chrome plated bumpers when exposed to extreme salt spray, humidity and thermal shock (minus 20 degrees to live steam. Bumper jack tests also put the urethane bumper in a favorable light.

OLDSMOBILE

RALLYE 350 - URETHANE COATED BUMPER

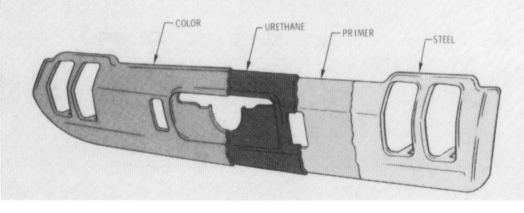

PLUS SALES

The pulling power of the Rallye 350 for showroom traffic can't be overemphasized. It has all the glamour to lure prospects. Then surround it with models considered most appealing to this type of customer . . . Cutlass, Cutlass S, Cutlass Supreme, Supreme SX, 4-4-2 . . . even Delta 88 models. Remember you have a car to suit the needs of almost everyone. Maybe it isn't the Rallye 350 but it's something close to it.

Don't waste a minute . . . put the Rallye 350 to work for you. It will sell itself. It will sell its sister models. It will be the BIG THING this spring for OLDSMOBILE.

In 1971, the auto industry in general turned its back on most factory involvement with high performance. This came largely because of the difficulty in meeting new Federal emission standards and, to a lesser degree, safety standards. The lag in the high performance area was obvious at Oldsmobile. The situation was depressed in general at Olds, in any event, as production totals of 558,889 saw the division slip to sixth place in the industry sales race.

The 4-4-2 cars remained a series in 1971, but were reduced to just a two-model line-up. Model 4487 was the $3,551 hardtop coupe that saw 6,285 sales. Model number 4467 was the $3,742 convertible. Only 1,304 were made. These two remaining 4-4-2 models suffered a large sales drop over the previous years and, for 1971, the pillared sports coupe was dropped completely.

Again this year, the 4-4-2 used a massive 455 cid V-8 engine for underhood kick. The velocity of that kick was greatly reduced, however, as the hp rating dropped to 270. If the 4-4-2 suffered in the "go" department for 1971, it retained many of its fine handling characteristics with the carry-over of the Rallye suspension system. Single white-stripe, wide-oval tires mounted on seven inch rims were part of the package along with dual exhausts, special emblems and stripes and Strato bucket seats.

Many general performance options remained this model year and most carried the famed "W" prefix. They included: W-25, the $157 dual-intake fiberglass hood; W-26, the $76 sports console with Hurst Dual Gate shifter; W-27, the $26 aluminum rear end cover; W-35, the $73 rear decklid spoiler; and W-37, the $99 heavy-duty two-plate clutch. Emission laws stripped the mighty W-31 option from the books in 1971, but a W-30 option was offered, although it did not achieve the performance level found in earlier W-30s. The W-30 for this year cost $369 and it was again built around a forced air induction 455 cid V-8. Horsepower rating dropped to 300. Special equipment included a heavy-duty air cleaner, aluminum intake manifold, sports mirrors, body stripes and special W-car emblems.

There was no doubt the 4-4-2 cars dropped in importance this year once the literature was studied. The main piece for this year was a full-color, full-line catalogue and the 4-4-2 had been de-emphasized. Overall, the Cutlass/F-85 intermediate group was becoming even more popular in the Oldsmobile model mix. The Cutlass Supreme became the lead car in the intermediate section of the catalogue. After the Cutlass S, the Cutlass and even the lowly budget F-85, the 4-4-2 was given a two page section near the back of the catalogue (see pages 98-99).*

*Front cover shown below.

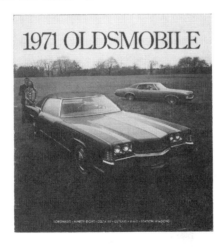

Those handsome, louvered Super Stock Wheels are available with argent trim, as shown. Or you can order them trimmed to match the body paint color you select. The 7-inch-wide, bias-belted white-stripe tires come standard.

4-4-2.

Turns drivers into enthusiasts.

With a special high-torque, 455-cubic-inch V-8, it's easily understandable. 4-4-2 performance is strictly top drawer. And we intend to *keep* it that way.

For 1971, we've increased the spark, opened up the breathing, and slipped in "a little more cam" just to make sure.

As for handling? The rest of the pack is still scrambling to match 4-4-2's special underpinnings, which include all heavy-duty components and stabilizer bars both *front and rear!*

Strato Bucket Seats, wide-striped louvered hood, Hurst Competition Shifter, heavy-duty wheels, and the super-wide bias-ply glass-belted tires with white stripes are also standard.

W-30: A special-performance package with factory-blueprinted engine! Available in 4-4-2 only. Includes lightweight fiberglass hood with functional air scoops and chromed hood pins. Special factory-blueprinted 455-CID, cold-air V-8 to help assure top performance. Performance-calibrated Quadrajet 4-bbl. carb. Special air-cleaner. High-overlap cam. Aluminum intake manifold. Hood and wide body-side paint stripes. Front disc brakes, manual. Lightweight sound insulation. Die-cast W-30 identification on front fenders. And, of course, dual sports-styled outside mirrors, raised-letter tires, and an anti-spin performance axle are a must! Order them along with your W-30 package.

The ultimate head-turning extra you can order. This lightweight fiberglass hood features functional dual air scoops, bold stripes, and special chromed exterior hood latches.

Can you think of a better way to set off your 4-4-2 instrument panel than with that handsome Custom-Sport Steering Wheel! It features a thick, pliable, leather-like vinyl grip and four brushed-metal spokes. Be sure to order one—along with a tach, clock, gauges, and other sporting extras.

We're playing your song! Through low-restriction full-dual exhausts with handsome flared outlets. They're standard. So is that exclusive and custom-notched rear bumper.

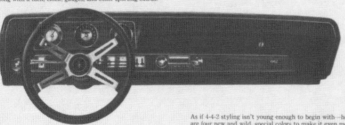

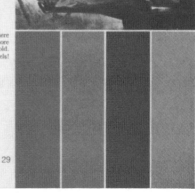

As if 4-4-2 styling isn't young enough to begin with—here are four new and wild, special colors to make it even more so! Viking Blue. Lime Green. Bittersweet. Saturn Gold. No extra charge—on 4-4-2, F-85, and all Cutlass models!

STANDARD ENGINE:
455 V-8 w/4-bbl. carburetor and dual exhausts
STANDARD TRANSMISSION:
Fully synchronized heavy-duty 3-speed manual with
Hurst Competition Shifter, floor-mounted

EXTERIOR DIMENSIONS: Coupe (In.)

Wheelbase	Length	Width	Height	Curb Weight
112.0	203.6	76.8	52.9	3792 lbs.

INTERIOR DIMENSIONS: Coupe (front/rear) (In.)

Headroom	Shoulder-room	Legroom	Trunk Capacity
37.9/36.3	58.2/57.7	41.5/32.3	17.0 cu. ft.

OTHER STANDARD FEATURES INCLUDE: Hood, body-side, and trunk-lid paint stripes. Louvered hood. Bucket seats. Low-restriction dual exhausts. Deluxe steering wheel. Wood-grain-vinyl instrument-panel trim. Concealed radio antenna. Recessed windshield wipers. Cigar lighter. FE2 (heavy-duty) suspension. G70 x 14" white-stripe wide-oval tires (bias-ply glass-belted). Heavy-duty 7-inch-wide wheels. Flo-Thru Ventilation.

Olds offers, at modest extra cost, a variety of accessories many of which are shown in the car illustrations, and may also be described on pages 36-37.

29

In 1972, the 4-4-2 package was dropped as a full series and returned to the status of an option. Oldsmobile made a rather dramatic move in the sales race, never-the-less, knocking long-time GM rival Pontiac out of its traditional third place niche in national sales with 758,711 cars.

The optional 4-4-2 package—option W-29—could be had on selected Cutlass, Cutlass S and Cutlass Supreme models. It was not offered this year in the budget F-85 series which by now consisted of just a single offering—a utilitarian town sedan. The 4-4-2 option cost from $71 to $150 depending upon what model was involved. It was labeled in the dealer book as an appearance and handling package—and it was no more than that. The package included the usual fare of decals, stripes, special emblems, hood louvers and heavy-duty suspension parts.

The W-30 had its last year as a meaningful performance option in 1972. The package centered on a 300 hp, 455 cid V-8 powerplant. Although it was the most powerful engine Olds built this year, it was down considerably compared to some of the more potent engines Olds had produced over the last decade. The W-30 package cost from $592 to $741, depending upon which series to which it was fitted. The option included: dual exhausts, forced air fiberglass hood, special stripes, heavy-duty radiator, front disc brakes and heavy-duty suspension and rear axle. In addition to op-

tions W-29 and W-30, a few performance options remained in the 1972 dealer book. They included: W-25, the $157 fiberglass hood; W-26, the $76 sports console; W-37, the $99 heavy-duty clutch; and W-39, the $42 Hurst shifter with manual three-speed transmission.

A Hurst/Olds returned to the Olds performance camp in 1972 and also served as official pace car for that year's Indianapolis 500. A total of 600 H/Os were built and they were divided between Cutlass Supreme coupes and convertibles. The familiar gold and white color pattern was used. A slightly warmed-over 455 V-8 was fitted along with heavy-duty suspension, dual exhausts, Hurst Dual Gate shifter and forced air hood. The H/O had a full option list with such toys as an electric sunroof, security alarm system and digital-read performance computer. Other H/O options included the W-30 performance package and a decal set identical to the ones worn by the pace car.

Despite its downgrading to option status, the 4-4-2 rated a two-page spread in the 1972 full-line color catalogue (see pages 102-103).* The W-30 performance option also rated a mention in this section. Hurst also put out an information sheet on its 1972 car (see pages 104-105)* along with press releases and photos on the actual Indy pace car (see page 106).

*Front covers shown below.

Strato-Bucket seats with centre console.

Cutlass instrument panel with Custom-sport steering wheel.

AVAILABLE WITH

Cutlass and Cutlass S Coupes and Cutlass Supreme Convertible

4-4-2 SPORTS/HANDLING PACKAGE (W29)
INCLUDES: Hood paint stripe. Hood louvers. Body striping. Blacked-out 4-4-2 grille. Chrome wheel-opening mouldings. Hurst Shifter 3-speed, floor-mounted, if standard transmission equipped with Rocket 350 V8. RALLYE SUSPENSION PACKAGE ALSO INCLUDED: Heavy-duty springs and shock absorbers, front and rear stabilizer bars, heavy-duty rear-suspension lower control arms 14" x 7" heavy-duty wheels.

W30 PERFORMANCE PACKAGE
INCLUDES: High-performance Rocket 455 V8 with 4-bbl carburetor and dual exhausts. High performance forced cold air induction system. Special camshaft. Heavy-duty radiator. Fiberglass hood with functional air scoops and tie-downs. Front wheel wide-oval tires with white raised letters, sports deck lid. Front anti-spin rear axle. REQUIRES Turbo Hydra-matic 400 transmission or 4-speed wide-ratio floor shift transmission.

OTHER ENGINES AVAILABLE
Rocket 350 V8, 2-bbl carburetor (L32). Rocket 350 V8, 4-bbl carburetor (L34). Rocket 455 V8 with dual exhausts (L75). Fiberglass hood also available with L34 or L75 engines.

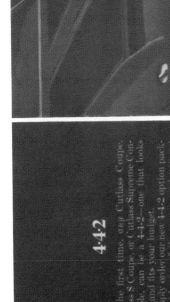

Fiberglass hood with functional scoops and tie-downs is included with the factory-blueprinted W30 Performance Package—and it's also available with 350 or 455 4-bbl. Rocket V8s.

Twin pipes are included when you order the Rocket 455 V8 or the W30 Performance Package. Other goodies to consider are Strato-Bucket Seats, Hurst 3-Speed Shifter, Custom-Sport Steering Wheel, etc., etc.

4-4-2

For the first time, any Cutlass Coupe, Cutlass S Coupe or Cutlass Supreme Convertible can be a 4-4-2—one that looks great and fits your budget.

Simply order our new 4-4-2 option package with any of these cars and you get the 4-4-2 transformation in two areas: looks and handling.

The looks starts with special paint striping on the hood and body. Then hood louvers. A special 4-4-2 grille. Chrome wheel-opening mouldings. And those magic 4-4-2 numbers on your car order.

The special handling package puts super-wide 14" x 7" heavy-duty wheels on the axles and beefed-up suspension components in the chassis. (Details below.)

For you you have three versions of Rocket V8s. And if you're a performance purist, there's still Dr. Oldsmobile's legendary W30 Package you can order.

Think about it—you, in a 4-4-2. Wow! Care to have your friends see you in the scene at left?

THE 1972 HURST/OLDS

Detroit, Mich.—The 1972 Hurst/Olds, recently named the official pace car for the Indianapolis '500' auto race, represents one of the few remaining domestic choices for the driver who values automotive performance. According to Robert F. Draper, president of Hurst Performance, Inc., the Warminster, Pa.-based producers of the special car, the Hurst/Olds was created to provide a broader definition of performance, incorporating engine response, handling, braking, driver comfort, styling, exclusivity and lasting value.

Offered in both hardtop coupe and convertible models, the Hurst/Olds is a limited-production conversion based on the Oldsmobile Cutlass Supreme. It is the latest in a line of such conversions produced by Hurst's specialty vehicle facility in Detroit, Mich. Currently in production, the Hurst/Olds will be available at Oldsmobile dealers across the country after March 1.

24175 Telegraph Road, Southfield, Mich. 48075
313—355-0160

 FACT SHEET

WHAT	Limited-production conversion based on the 1972 Oldsmobile Cutlass Supreme in hardtop coupe or convertible models.
PURPOSE	To provide true, all-around performance through better engine response, handling, braking, driver comfort, styling, exclusivity and lasting value.

STANDARD EQUIPMENT
- Cameo White body color only
- Hurst Custom Laser Stripe in Hurst Gold
- Black Accents (grille, hood scoops, head- and taillight bezels)
- Twin Sports Mirrors in body color
- Vinyl Landau Roof in antique gold
- Goodyear Polysteel Tires, G60x14
- Super Stock III Wheels in Hurst Gold
- 455 CID Performance Engine
- 3.23 rear axle ratio
- Power Disc Brakes
- Rallye Suspension

OPTIONAL EQUIPMENT
- Hurst Electric Sun Roof with integral wind deflector
- Hurst Digital Performance Computer
- Hurst Auto Security Alarm System
- Hurst Wheel-Guard Sentry
- Hurst Indianapolis '500' Pace Car Replica Decal Set
- W-30 High-Performance Engine with heavy-duty cooling system, 3.42 rear axle, anti-spin differential

AVAILABILITY See it at your local Oldsmobile Dealership after March first.

24175 Telegraph Road, Southfield, Mich. 48075

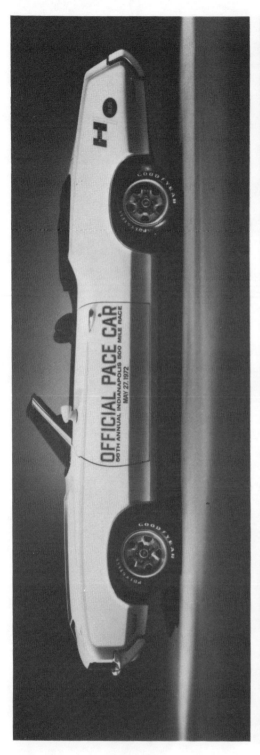

Olds held a solid third in industry sales standings in 1973 with an all-time sales high of 938,970. High performance continued to fade, however, and the 4-4-2 was an option available only on coupes from the Cutlass and Cutlass S series.

Cutlass styling was dramatically revised this model year and its acceptance from the buying public was one of the big reasons for Olds' increased sales volume. The new styling treatment looked sharp with the 4-4-2 trim, too. For this model year, the 4-4-2 was strictly an appearance and handling option. It was listed as option W-29—the only "W" prefix option listed in the dealer book. Cost was $121 on the Cutlass models and $58 on the Cutlass S. This included various body side and decklid stripes, special louvered hood and grille and the FE-2 heavy-duty Rallye suspension package. A new Salon (V1-M) package was offered on Cutlass S and Cutlass Supreme models, also. It was a mild attempt at a touring sedan. It cost $192 and offered special suspension components tuned to a new type of steel belted radial tires.

A Hurst/Olds was available this year and again the new Cutlass styling package looked great. This was the most potent car from the Olds camp and a bit higher performance 455 cid V-8 could be ordered on non-air conditioned examples. Base car was the Cutlass S coupe. Body color was either Ebony Black or Cameo White with gold stripes and body accents. Standard H/O equipment included: twin sport mirrors, a landau style half-roof, Super Stock wheels, special hood ornament and unique rear quarter windows with the H/O emblem. Other components included the Rallye suspension, power front disc brakes, 455 cid V-8 engine, wet-look vinyl swivel bucket front seats and a console topped with a Hurst Dual Gate shifter. The Hurst/Olds was available in Olds showrooms by April, 1973, and sales for the model run totalled 1,097.

The 4-4-2 package rated only a small mention on a single page in the 1973 full-line color catalogue (see page 108).* Hurst, on the other hand, put out a nice, oversize color folder covering its 1973 model (see pages 109-113).* Hurst/Olds photos appear on page 114.

*Front covers shown below.

Like bucket seats? Cutlass S has something special available on the opposite page—high-backed buckets of solid foam, upholstered in Espana-grained Morocceen with a new "wet-look." They're sleek, they're contoured—and they swivel! Offered in black, white, green, cranberry red or saddle.

The new Cutlass S panel floodlights the controls at night. New mist-control gives you a single wipe of the windshield when needed. Panel units are easily removed to simplify servicing when it's needed. And if you like a still sportier look, order the Custom Sport steering wheel.

This is the standard Cutlass S seat with new comfort for two—or three. Lagoon cloth in wedge-wood blue, or beige. Or in Morocceen in black, white, green, cranberry red or saddle.

Touch a lever, and this seat swivels out to meet you, swivels you neatly into place behind the wheel. Yet it's also adjustable for your comfort behind the wheel. Available only in Cutlass S.

4-4-2 is alive and well! The basic 4-4-2 Package (W29) gets you a car that is set apart in ride and handling. (Details at right.)

Inside story on the Cutlass S: Under the great new look, there's a great new ride on a 112-inch wheelbase. It feels smoother, more like a bigger, heavier car—because the new suspension system has been patterned after our bigger Oldsmobiles. You'll enjoy new comfort, too, on seats of solid foam up to six inches thick. You have new room to stretch out, in practically every dimension. You can even order our new Vista Vent in the roof. Most of all, you'll have a sweet and sporty coupe that's every inch an Oldsmobile.

MODEL AVAILABILITY: Cutlass S Colonnade Hardtop Coupe

STANDARD ENGINE: Rocket 350 V8 with 4-bbl. carburetor

STANDARD TRANSMISSION: Fully synchronized 3-speed manual with column shift

EXTERIOR DIMENSIONS: (in.)

Wheelbase	Length	Width	Height	Curb Weight (lbs.)
112.0	207.0	76.5	53.3	3840

INTERIOR DIMENSIONS: (front/rear) (in.)

Headroom	Shoulder-room	Legroom
37.7/37.0	59.6/57.5	42.1/33.7

OTHER STANDARD FEATURES INCLUDE: Deluxe Armrests (Front and Rear). Front Disc Brakes. Cigar Lighter. Wall-to-Wall Carpeting. Interior-Operated Hood Lock. Rocker-Panel and Wheel-Opening Moldings. Windshield Radio Antenna. Seat Lap Belts (3 Front and 3 Rear). Seat Shoulder Belts (2 Front). Flow-Thru Ventilation. Flex-Head Intake Valves. Valve Rotators. Deluxe Steering Wheel.

OTHER AVAILABLE OPTIONS INCLUDE: Tinted Glass. Power Windows. Power Trunk-Lid Release. Vista Vent Roof Ventilator. Power Door Locks. Protective-Side Moldings with Vinyl Inserts. Vinyl Rooftop Covering. Rear-Window Defogger. Air Conditioner. Combination Dome and Reading Lamp. Remote-Control Outside Rearview Mirror. Sports-Styled Mirrors Color-Styled to Body. Sports Console. Mini Storage Console. Two-Tone Paint. Anti-Spin Rear Axle. Power Brakes (with discs up front). Engine Block Heater. Rocket 445 V8 with 4-bbl. carburetor. 4-Speed Floor-Shift Wide-Ratio Transmission. Turbo Hydra-matic Transmission. Dual Exhaust System. Tilt-Away Steering Wheel. Custom-Sport Steering Wheel. Vari-Ratio Power Steering. Super Stock II Wheels. Super Stock III Wheels. Chrome Wheel Discs. White-Stripe Tires. Instrument Panel Gauges. Electric Clock. Radio. Bumper Rub Strip (Front and Rear). Bumper Guards (Front and Rear) with Vinyl Inserts. 4-4-2 Appearance and Handling Package. Paint-Stripe Decals. Outside Temperature Indicator. Heavy-Duty Suspension. Trailer Wiring Harness. Stereo Tape Player.

4-4-2 APPEARANCE AND HANDLING PACKAGE (W29) INCLUDES: Body-side and deck-lid decal, 4-4-2 radiator grille, black hood louvers, grille and deck-lid numbers, plus rocker-panel and wheel-opening moldings. Rallye suspension package (also included): heavy-duty front and rear stabilizer bars; and heavy-duty rear-suspension upper control arms. 14 x 7" wheels. Available with any Rocket V8 engine. Cutlass or Cutlass S Coupe models only

35

THE 1973 HURST/OLDS
Designed and Built Exclusively For The Man In Motion.

For the particular individual who values true automotive excellence, Hurst Performance Inc. designs and produces the 1973 limited-production conversion Hurst/Olds.

Based on the popular, newly-styled Oldsmobile Cutlass S, the spirited character of this distinctive automobile is evidenced in both styling and performance, incorporating engine response, handling, braking, driver comfort, styling, exclusivity, and lasting value, the Hurst/Olds offers a full complement of standard and optional features

designed to produce spirited, stylish, safe motoring. Exclusive styling is characterized by the Hurst gold body striping, custom blacked-out taillight bezels and grille with leading edges accented in silver, Nassau styled hood ducts, special Super Stock III wheels, and Landau roof with opera windows, in Cameo White or Ebony Black, color-coordinated twin sports mirrors, add to the spirited look. A classic Oldsmobile Hood Ornament lends additional flair to the styling of this exclusive automobile. To preserve the lasting value of your

Hurst/Olds, standard black rubber bumper steps protect the finish.

Every Hurst/Olds is engineered to produce the performance. Its spirited styling implies. The basic powerplant is the proven 455 CID L75 Performance Engine, supported by power disc brakes, Rallye suspension, dual exhausts with custom chrome outlets, and a Center console with Hurst Dual/Gate transmission shift control. All of these standard equipment features have been incorporated for the flexibility of acceleration, handling and performance, they provide.

Standard on non-air conditioned cars only

The 455 CID L77 Performance Engine is available featuring special cam shaft, special intake manifold with high speed torque converter and 3.23 axle rear axle (rear axle ratio is 3.08 on air conditioned cars) to provide the perfect package for those who desire something special in engine power and performance.

For its reputation for automotive excellence, the Hurst/Olds features the B. F. Goodrich Lifesaver Radial T/A, the only race-proven street tire, as

standard equipment this year. It is the only domestically manufactured passenger tire to satisfy both Department of Transportation requirements for highway use and be approved by the Sports Car Club of America for track competition. It was the first street tire to finish a major international endurance race in modern times. Another first in modern racing history, the Radial T/A took the pole position in the GTO class at the 1972 running of the 24 hours of LeMans. Designed to provide optimum handling characteristics under wet and dry highway conditions, it also offers superior tread mileage. The T/A is cool running, gives superior high speed performance, and improved all weather handling, compared to other 60 series tires. All of these features meet Hurst/Olds high standards.

A selected list of special options are available for the true performance enthusiast.

The Digital Tachometer allows the Hurst/Olds performance enthusiast to monitor engine RPM's in hundreds of revolutions per minute continuously. Equipped with a memory system, this digital tachometer can be referred to or reset at any time

Offering optimum protection, the Auto Security Alarm System was designed to safeguard the owner's investment in this special automobile. Electronic relays at hood, doors and trunk warn of attempted entry by triggering a siren (California cars are equipped with a bell). This option also includes a mercury-operated trunk light which operates the siren through electronic impulses.

Solutions to the problem of wheel and tire security have ranged from the ineffective to the bizarre. Now Hurst offers a simple highly effective solution with the optional Hurst Loc/Lug. The superiority of this security Loc/Lug is due to a special shape and wrenching method rather than the normal hex shape which can be easily removed.

Standard or optional, every Hurst styling and performance feature has been designed exclusively for the Hurst/Olds by Hurst Performance Inc. to produce the truly high performance automobile that the man in motion desires.

1. The custom touch of yesteryear, every Hurst/Olds fold-down Hood Ornament, designed exclusively for this special car adds additional flair to today's distinctive styling.

2. Of course, the Hurst Dual/Gate shifter is standard on the Hurst/Olds. This special shifter gives the driver the choice between normal automatic transmission control or a performance controlled shift pattern.

3. 4. The distinctive touch ... opera windows with mylar etching of the Hurst/Olds insignia add a very special styling accent to the Landau styled padded half-top look on the black car. In addition, these wet-look coach-roof the black car with Bright stainless steel moldings and a double welt sets this particular car apart from all the others.

5. For the performance enthusiast, the optional Digital Tachometer reads out engine RPM in hundreds of revolutions per minute, continuously monitors engine RPM and stores the highest RPM it sees. A memory system stores the RPM recorded which can be displayed on command and be easily reset at any time.

6. Featured on every Hurst/Olds are special Super Stock III wheels ... Hurst gold on the Cameo White car or Black on the Ebony Black car. This year, Hurst/Olds introduces the B F Goodrich Lifesaver Radial T/A tire, as standard equipment. It's the radial street tire that goes to the races, having already proved its superior performance at Daytona, Watkins Glen, Sebring, and Le Mans as well as B F Goodrich proving grounds. These Radial T/A's grab the road and hold it through twists and turns as well as straightaways, giving excellent traction on both wet and dry surfaces. In addition, these Radial T/A's offer superior tread mileage, performance comfort, handling, and stability.

7. Another custom touch exclusive chrome tail pipes not only add to its appearance but contribute a deep, throaty sound that reflects the superb performance of this unique automobile.

8. The optional Hurst Loc/Lug provides security you can count on for your B F Goodrich tires and Super Stock III wheels. It utilizes a special shape and wrenching method in place of the usual easily removable hex shape.

9. Rich leather seats are not only handsome but offer the extra convenience of swivel mobility.

The Ebony Black swivel seat features a wet look panel which complements the black vinyl half-top wet look roof

10. There is no question that the Hurst/Olds is an exclusive automobile. Its unique styling readily identifies it as something special, while the distinctive emblems on the deck-lid and console insure its prestigious identification.

11. The Nassau-styled duct in Hurst gold is another distinctive styling 'flair' that quickly identifies this very individual automobile.

12. The Hurst Super Air Shock is the first really new air shock since the first air shock. Its special construction puts it a cut above all the others because it was built just for your kind of performance.

13. In Cameo White of Ebony Black, this racy interior reflects the Hurst image, and offers comfort and convenience. High-back swivel bucket seats are separated by a standard console and Hurst Dual/Gate shifter. Identifying emblem on the wrap-around console adds to the Hurst distinction. The console also contains the optional digital tachometer.

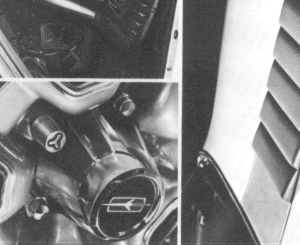

Standard Equipment

* Vinyl Landau New Half Top
* Hurst Dual Gate Shifter
* B F Goodrich Lifesaver Radial T A Tires GR60x14
* Super Stock III Wheels in Hurst Gold
  and Ebony Black
* Hurst Custom Gold Body Accents
* Classic Osterdrive Hood Ornament
* Small Quarter Windows with H-O Mylar Etching
* Nassau Hood Duct
* Custom Chrome Tail Pipes
* 455 CID L77 Performance Engine
  and Transmission Package
* Ebony Black or Cameo White body color
* Black Accents grille taillight bezels)
* Twin Sports Mirrors in body color
* Swivel Seats
* Power Disc Brakes
* Rallye Suspension

Optional Equipment

* Hurst Digital Tachometer
* Hurst LocLugs
* Hurst Auto Security Alarm System
* Hurst Super Air Shocks

HURST
PERFORMANCE
INC.

10711 NORTHEND AVE.,
FERNDALE, MICHIGAN 48220

Again in 1974, the 4-4-2 option was offered but it was strictly an appearance and handling package. A Hurst/Olds was available this year, though, and it was the official Indianapolis 500 pace car for the third time in the decade. In general, Olds once again hung onto the hotly contested third place in industry sales standings by virtue of 619,168 sales.

Option W-29, the 4-4-2 package, cost $58 on the Cutlass S and $121 on the Cutlass. The package included: decklid and grille numerals, hood louvers, other decals and stripes and a special handling system. Big news in the Cutlass camp this year was the revised Salon package offered on the Cutlass Supreme group. It again centered around steel belted radial tires and a specially tuned suspension system. Option Y-78 listed for $361 and also featured special interior trim, contour reclining bucket seats, console and dimmer switch built into the turn signal lever. The car was definitely a response to the growing popularity of European touring sedans in this country.

The Hurst/Olds provided the last hope for Olds buyers seeking a bit more performance. Actually, three types of conversions were built by Hurst in 1974. Since the production Cutlass convertible had been gone for two years and an open car was thought essential to pacing the 500, a special open Cutlass convertible (actually a pair of them) was built. A second production Hurst/Olds, based on the Cutlass coupe, was created. The W-30 designation was cleverly revived for use on this model. Standard equipment here included: heavy-duty suspension, modified automatic transmission, Super Stock 15 inch wheels and a 455 cid V-8 with dual exhausts. Options included: a digital tachometer, wheel locks, chromed mud guards and a security alarm system. The color again was white with gold-and-black trim. The third Hurst-produced conversion was an 88 convertible built in limited numbers. The author served as Oldsmobile public relations representative for the 1974 pace car project.

A special color folder featuring the production Hurst/Olds and the Indy pace car was printed in 1974 (see pages 117-124),* along with press releases and press photos on the pace machine. The full-line color catalogue included a small segment on the 4-4-2 (see page 116).*

*Front covers shown below.

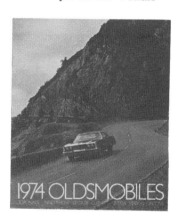

This is what the Cutlass S Coupe looks like if you don't order buckets. In Logan cloth in blue or saddle, or in Morocceen of black, cranberry, white, green or beige.

Inside, a Cutlass doesn't remind you of the modest price you paid. Smart Lansing nylon in blue or saddle; all-Morocceen upholstery in black, green or white.

Touch a lever and this seat swivels out to meet you, swivels you neatly into the car.

How to make a Cutlass or Cutlass S Coupe still sportier? Give it the famous 4-4-2 treatment, with special suspension and markings. Your Olds salesman has the details.

Even the briefest look, the shortest round-the-block ride, will tell you why Cutlass brings more new people into the Olds family than any other series.

Sleek, agile, roomy, modestly priced—Cutlass has a special appeal when you discover how easily you can step up to all the virtues of an Oldsmobile.

The sedan puts four doors and family-size room on a 116-inch wheelbase. The coupe puts a sporty fastback look on a 112-inch wheelbase.

Whichever Cutlass you choose, you get lots of standard equipment. Rocket V8, of course. Front disc brakes. Power steering. And automatic transmission.

But there's more. A soft-grip vinyl-covered steering wheel. Deep-foam seats. A Swingaway grille that's hinged to swing back when the bumper gets bumped. And thick vinyl impact strips on the bumpers, front and rear.

Now, if coupes are your style—and the sportier, the better—Cutlass S has a lot to offer. It has a distinctive grille. Neat parking lamps sculptured into the panels on each side. Chrome accents on rocker panels and wheel openings. Cut-pile carpeting on floors and lower door panels. And those great swivel buckets are available only in the S.

You can see Cutlass and Cutlass S have a lot to help you feel "Drivehappy" this year.

CUTLASS STANDARD FEATURES INCLUDE: Rocket 350 V8 with cold-air induction system, improved starter. Turbo Hydra-matic transmission. Power steering. Disc-type front brakes. New soft-grip steering wheel. Grained wood appearance on doors and instrument panel. Hydraulic bumper systems, front and rear, with vinyl impact strips. New combination seat/shoulder belts (self-storing) with starter interlock, for driver and right front passenger.
CUTLASS S FEATURES ALSO INCLUDE: Chrome hood molding; chrome rocker panel and wheel-opening moldings. Swingaway grille with flanking parking lights. Cut-pile carpeting.
SPECIFICATIONS (SEDAN/COUPE): Wheelbase, 116/112 in. Length, 214.6/211.5 in. Height, 56.1/53.4 in. Approximate curb weight, 4040/3984 lbs. Luggage space, 16.0/16.0 cu. ft.
AVAILABLE OPTIONS AND ACCESSORIES INCLUDE: Vinyl top. Super Stock wheels. Steel-belted radial tires. 4-4-2 package (coupe), including special suspension and handling components. Power brakes (disc-type, front). Rocket 455 V8. Dual exhaust system. Anti-spin rear axle. AM/FM stereo radio. Stereo tape player. Four-season air conditioning. Vista Vent (Coupes). Sports mirrors. Also see pages 44-47.

CUTLASS COLONNADE HARDTOP COUPE

When you can get this much room and this much class in a Cutlass Sedan—for less than you'd pay for a lot of other cars—it's no wonder Car and Driver readers voted the '73 Cutlass "best family sedan" last year.

35

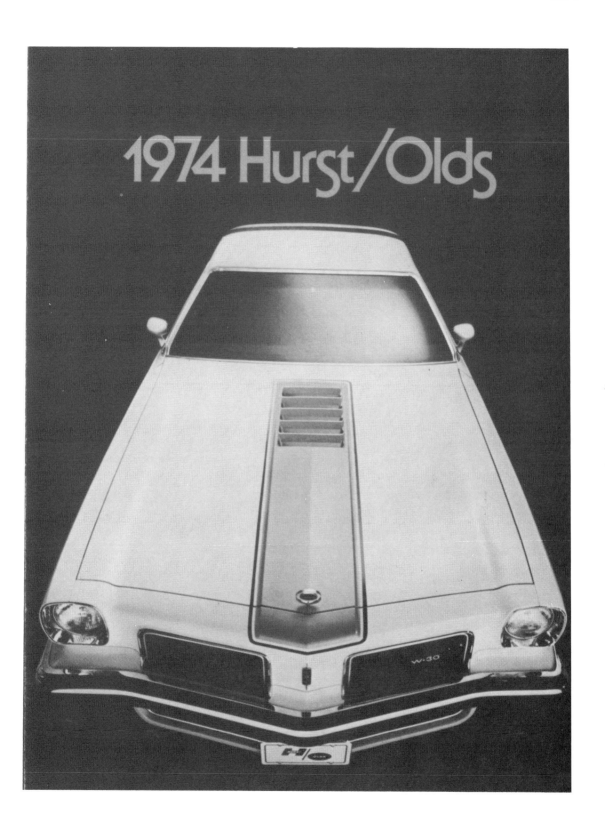

1974 Hurst/Olds Offic

Fully Padded Vinyl Top with Contrasting Simulated Roll Bar Insert

Modified Rear Quarter Window

Recessed Hurst/Olds Exterior Emblem

15 x 7 Super Stock III Wheels

H70 x 15 Raised White Letter Wide Oval Tires

Dual Color Keyed Sport Mirrors

W-30 Engine Identification

Optional Hurst Molded Splash Guards

Optional Hurst Loc/Lugs

ial Pace Car

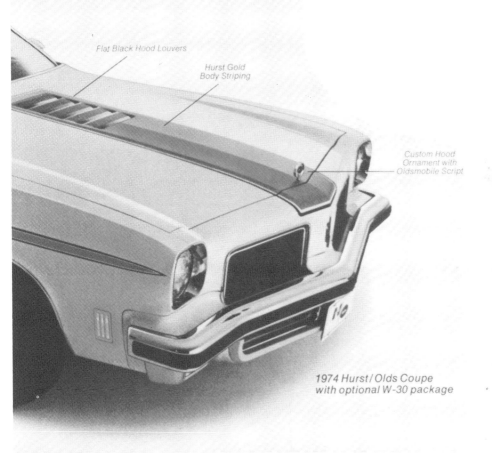

Flat Black Hood Louvers

Hurst Gold
Body Striping

Custom Hood
Ornament with
Oldsmobile Script

1974 Hurst/Olds Coupe
with optional W-30 package

Dual Exhaust

Color Coordinated
Accent Mouldings

Optional
Hurst/Olds License Plates

additional W-30* features

Rallye Suspension
Dual Snorkel Air Cleaner
Custom Sport Steering Wheel
Heavy Duty Cooling
Sport Console
Performance Turbo Hydramatic
400 Transmission
Power Front Disc Brakes
Instrumentation Gauge Package
High Energy Ignition

*Not available in California.
Y-77 (350 c.i.) appearance package
standard in California and also
available in all cars.

Cameo white body with black vinyl top and white roll bar insert.

Ebony black body with black vinyl top and white roll bar insert.

Ebony black body with white vinyl top and black roll bar insert.

features

Included with the W-30 performance package is the proven Hurst Dual/Gate automatic shifter mounted in an Oldsmobile sport console. Dual shift patterns provide the ultimate in street/strip control.

Swivel bucket seats are the newest way to provide arm chair driving comfort combined with easy entry and exit. Standard on all Hurst/Oldsmobiles.

Motor Minder Economy Gauge provides timely engine efficiency read outs. Monitoring manifold vacuum enables more economical driving habits and efficiency.

For wheel/tire security, optional Hurst Loc/Lugs provide simple operating tamper proof protection. Hurst color molded splash guards are made from high impact plastic to eliminate rust, corrosion, rattles, and paint deterioration. They provide fender protection and retain a pleasant appearance.

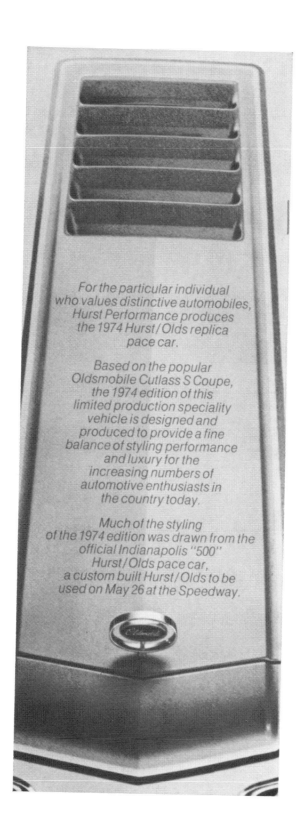

For the particular individual
who values distinctive automobiles,
Hurst Performance produces
the 1974 Hurst/Olds replica
pace car.

Based on the popular
Oldsmobile Cutlass S Coupe,
the 1974 edition of this
limited production speciality
vehicle is designed and
produced to provide a fine
balance of styling performance
and luxury for the
increasing numbers of
automotive enthusiasts in
the country today.

Much of the styling
of the 1974 edition was drawn from the
official Indianapolis "500"
Hurst/Olds pace car,
a custom built Hurst/Olds to be
used on May 26 at the Speedway.

1974 Hurst/Olds Coupe with optional Indianapolis "500" pace car Decal Kit.

Oldsmobile performance enthusiasts had both a 4-4-2 and Hurst/Olds package in 1975. The division continued to do well, too, in the industry sales race and grabbed third place on the strength of 628,720 sales.

The Cutlass and Cutlass S coupes could again be fitted with option W-29—the "4-4-2 appearance and handling package." It was available with any engine selection. The package included: front fender and decklid numerals, special grille and hood louvers, body side and trunk decals and the special FE-2 Rallye suspension option. Cost was $61 on the Cutlass S and $128 on the Cutlass models.

Olds had offered a Hurst/Olds in consecutive model years from 1972 through this year. The 1975 H/O again was based on a Cutlass coupe. Either white or black exteriors were decorated with gold striping with either white or black interior trim. The W-25 version of the H/O was fitted with the L-34 350 cid motor and smaller Turbo-Hydramatic 350, while the W-30 was powered by the more potent L-74 455 cid motor hooked to a Turbo-Hydramatic 400. Standard equipment included: special grille and hood, sports mirrors, Super Stock III wheels painted in Hurst Gold, raised letter radial tires, swivel bucket seats, console with Hurst Dual Gate shifter, Hurst Hatch roof, padded half-top, special interior and exterior emblems and W-25 or W-30 fender identification. The standard H/O package cost $1,095 over the base price of the Cutlass it was built from. Extra cost exclusive H/O options included: splash guards, wheel locks, special tachometer and auto alarm system. Production totals for the 1975 H/O were 2,535.

In the 1975 color full-line catalogue, the 4-4-2 rated a small corner of a Cutlass S page (see page 126).* There was also a Hurst/Olds press kit (see pages 127-130) and a folder.

*Front cover shown below.

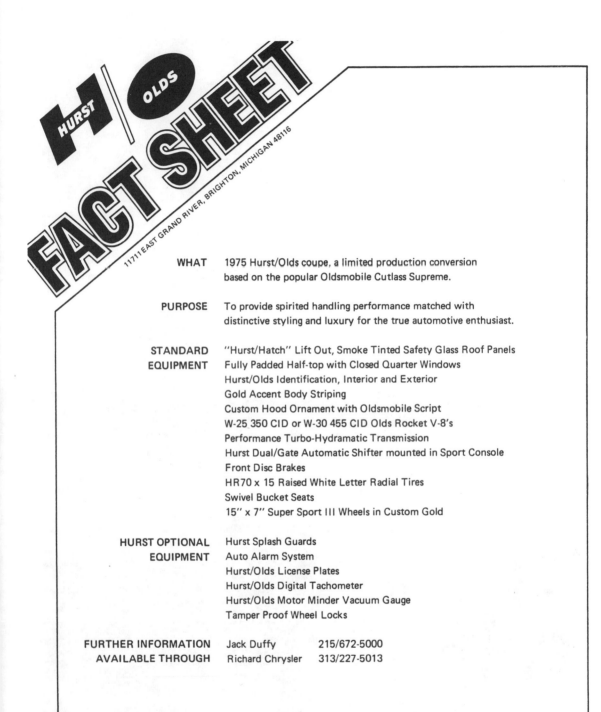

HURST/OLDS FACT SHEET

11711 EAST GRAND RIVER, BRIGHTON, MICHIGAN 48116

WHAT 1975 Hurst/Olds coupe, a limited production conversion based on the popular Oldsmobile Cutlass Supreme.

PURPOSE To provide spirited handling performance matched with distinctive styling and luxury for the true automotive enthusiast.

STANDARD EQUIPMENT
"Hurst/Hatch" Lift Out, Smoke Tinted Safety Glass Roof Panels
Fully Padded Half-top with Closed Quarter Windows
Hurst/Olds Identification, Interior and Exterior
Gold Accent Body Striping
Custom Hood Ornament with Oldsmobile Script
W-25 350 CID or W-30 455 CID Olds Rocket V-8's
Performance Turbo-Hydramatic Transmission
Hurst Dual/Gate Automatic Shifter mounted in Sport Console
Front Disc Brakes
HR70 x 15 Raised White Letter Radial Tires
Swivel Bucket Seats
15" x 7" Super Sport III Wheels in Custom Gold

HURST OPTIONAL EQUIPMENT
Hurst Splash Guards
Auto Alarm System
Hurst/Olds License Plates
Hurst/Olds Digital Tachometer
Hurst/Olds Motor Minder Vacuum Gauge
Tamper Proof Wheel Locks

FURTHER INFORMATION AVAILABLE THROUGH
Jack Duffy   215/672-5000
Richard Chrysler   313/227-5013

11711 EAST GRAND RIVER, BRIGHTON, MICHIGAN 48116

TO BE RELEASED FEBRUARY 20, 1975

Detroit, Michigan — The 1975 Hurst/Olds coupe represents one of the few remaining limited production specialty vehicles designed for automotive enthusiasts who value true automotive excellence. According to William Kay, president of Hurst Performance, Inc., co-producers of the car, the Hurst/Olds is designed to provide a fine balance of luxury, styling, performance, and lasting value for the individual who demands more than transportation from his automobile.

The 1975 H/O will be based on the Oldsmobile Cutlass Supreme and will be offered in both white and black coupes. The conversion will take place at the Hurst Specialty Vehicle Division facility in Brighton, Michigan. This latest version of the H/O line marks the 6th year Hurst and Oldsmobile have jointly produced the vehicle from which they have both enjoyed enormous sales success and customer acceptance since the first 1968 H/O was announced.

For those who have been frustrated lately with the intermediate convertible shortage, the Hurst/Olds introduces the best of both worlds with the New Hurst/Hatch roof. The Hurst/Hatches are smoke tinted, molded safety glass panels which secure into a fabricated framework within the roof line. When removed, exciting open air motoring results while the panels are neatly stored in a case in the trunk compartment. This Hurst/Hatch concept patterns expensive sports car design incorporating strength, safety, styling as well as refreshing sunshine driving.

Powerplants for 1975 include two versions of Oldsmobile Rocket V-8's, the W-30 455 CID, and the W-25 350 CID engines. Both are mated to the proven performance model Turbo-Hydramatic automatic transmission

(more)

and are controlled by the famous Hurst Dual/Gate shifter. W-30 features
include power disc brakes and variable ratio power steering. Radial tires are
mounted on 7'' wide gold Super Sport III wheels, providing spirited
handling, braking, and performance — a trait common to all H/O's since
their inception.

Styling highlights include traditional gold accent striping and a fully
padded half-top trimmed in stainless molding. The rear quarter windows have
been closed to provide the distinguished landau appearance. Swivel bucket
seats, dual sport mirrors, and interior and exterior H/O identification mark
this year's edition distinctively, mating the styling and performance into
one exclusive package.

Truly the finest edition of a classic in its own time, the 1975 Hurst/Olds;
available at Olds dealers nationwide in early March.

(30)

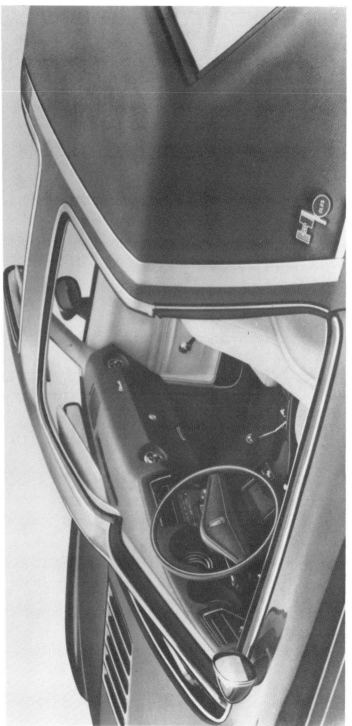

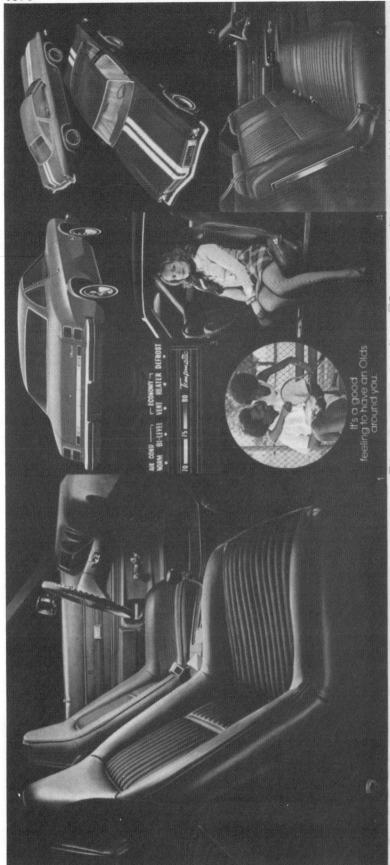

It's a good feeling to have an Olds around you

① Like to sport it up? Then order your Olds Cutlass S with swivel bucket seats and sports console. Touch a lever and the seat swings out to welcome you. Very convenient. Available in luxurious Repose cloth or handsome all-vinyl. (Top) Cutlass S Colonnade Hardtop Coupe.

② Fastback styling adds a look of action. ③ Tempmatic air conditioning now available. Includes an economy setting for best economy. ④ Available swivel bucket seat in action! ⑤ Available 4-4-2 option includes those special stripes, louvered hood, name plate and Rallye suspension. ⑥ Standard Coupe interior in choice of vinyl or cloth.

What's the "S" stand for? Sport! Spirit! Swagger! Take your pick. With that youthful fastback styling; smooth, agile handling; and spritely performance—Cutlass S fits all three!

Care to young-it-up still more? Then order away. Bucket seats that swivel, center console, sport mirrors, custom sport steering wheel and super stock sport wheels are all available.

So is the famous 4-4-2 package with special striping, louvered hood and its own suspension components.

Imagine, you in a sporty Cutlass S! It can happen. Easily. Because with all its winning ways, Cutlass S is still priced with many cars that carry a low-price name.

No wonder Cutlass S has helped move so many people up to Olds quality and value.

CUTLASS S SPECIFICATIONS & STANDARD POWER TEAM (COUPE). Wheelbase, 112 inches. Length, 211.7 inches. Engine 250.6-cvl (1-bbl Transmission, 3-speed manual, fully synchronized Rear axle ratio, 2.73

CUTLASS S STANDARD EQUIPMENT. Full-foam bench seats. Power steering. Front disc brakes. French-Walnut wood-grained applique trim. Interior-operated hood release. GM specification steel-belted radial-ply

tires. Flo-Thru Ventilation. High-energy ignition system. Reduced maintenance schedule. Catalytic converter. Bumper Impact strips and hydraulic bumper system, front and rear. Deluxe steering wheel. Cigar lighter. And more.

CUTLASS S AVAILABLE EQUIPMENT. 260 V8 2-bbl. engine. 350 V8 4-bbl. engine. 455 V8 4-bbl. engine. Full-vinyl roof. Till-away steering wheel. Custom sport steering wheel with soft grip. Locking fuel cap. Air

conditioner. Tinted glass. Power door locks. Power windows. Power trunk-lid release. Vista Vent roof. Coupe. Protective side moldings. Automatic cruise control. Fuel economy gauge. Rallye suspension package. Anti-spin axle. Chrome wheel covers. Headlamp-on reminder. Turbo Hydra-matic transmission. And more.

Third place was beginning to be a habit with Oldsmobile and it was again secured in 1976 with sales totals of 874,618. The Olds performance machines remained in the doldrums, though.

Again, option W-29 was there and, again, it was confined to just a handling and appearance package. The rectangular headlights were the main new feature of the Cutlass and they blended nicely with the 4-4-2 decaling and stripes. The W-29 option cost $134.

With the performance of the 4-4-2 offerings at best marginal, there were several other 1976 models that still caused mild stirrings from the performance oriented Olds buyers. These included the Cutlass Salon, Starfire SX and GT, and the Omega SX.

Most popular options that had even been remotely associated with high performance had been removed from the dealer order book and replaced with items like a five-speed manual overdrive transmission and dash-mounted fuel economy meter.

Olds printed a separate color catalogue for the 1976 Cutlass, Omega and Starfire. It gave the bottom third of a Cutlass S page to the 4-4-2 option (see page 134).*

*Front cover shown below.

What smooth, aerodynamic styling can do for you in the air. Olds Cutlass S can do for your spirit on the road.

For 1975, Cutlass S lines are sleek and more uninhibited than ever. The new grille in that all-new front end, for example. It starts out like a usual grille, then slants back with a flair all its own. These headlamps, too, are new. They're rectangular.

The new side styling— smooth like a fuselage. To the rear—a gently sloping fast-back roofline that says "Let's buckle up and go!"

And when you do, you find the going smooth and quick. Standard power steering and a trim 112-inch wheelbase help make handling and parking a driver's delight.

A lot of mid-size car? To be sure. Yet even with all its sporty good looks and care-free flair, Cutlass S is still priced with cars that carry low price names. And that good friends, can keep you feeling carefree, too!

Cutlass S, Colonnade Hardtop Coupe (left). Sporty, spirited, low priced.

1. Available swivel bucket seats that swing out to greet you. (Console available, at extra cost). A bench seat is standard.

2. Cutlass S with available 4-4-2 package, low price point striper. 4-4-2 decals. FE2 rally suspension.

3. Sporty 5-speed manual transmission available. The fifth gear is overdrive for efficiency.

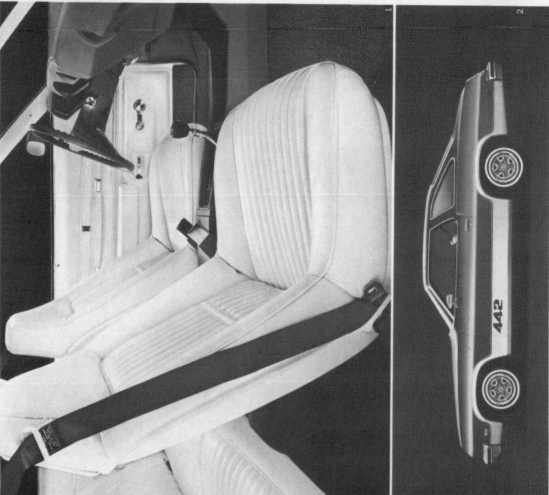

Model year 1977 was a boom year for the automobile industry and its third place seller—Oldsmobile—cashed in with sales totals of 1,135,909. This was the first time Olds had moved into the million car annual production club normally reserved for Ford and Chevrolet. (In fact, Olds is still the only make other than the "Big Two" to crack that barrier.)

The W-29 handling and appearance option—the 4-4-2—again could be ordered. This year the price tag was $169. There were a couple of other packages that might have caused a performance buyer to take a second peek at Olds in 1977. These models included the sporty Starfire GT and the Cutlass Salon. In a difficult-to-understand move, after three Cutlass pace cars had been used over the last decade, Oldsmobile provided a Delta 88 Indianapolis pace car in 1977.

The 4-4-2 was accorded a bit more color catalogue space in 1977 with a unique photo of a current 4-4-2 strategically placed in front of a one-stall garage housing a Futuramic Rocket 88 coupe (see page 136).*

*Front cover shown below.

Cutlass 4.4.2

There's still a car around that turns corners as easily as it turns heads. And it's still called — 4-4-2!

Since the original in '65, 4-4-2 has earned a reputation among enthusiasts for performance, crisp handling and nobody-like-me looks!

As you can see—the legend lives on! No dainty pin stripes for this available 4-4-2 package. Instead, bold stripes and special grille to complement that sleek fastback exterior.

And what would a 4-4-2 be without a hefty choice of power plants? So pick and choose. A spunky 231 V6 comes standard.

Prefer your spirit V8-style? There's an available 260 V8 with a 5-speed manual shifter. Still more cubes? You've got them. Our famous Rocket 350 4-barrel V8 or our new Rocket 403 4-barrel V8 with Turbo Hydra-matic—are available.

Bucket seats, sports console and more—also available to help make your 4-4-2 fit as snug as a driving glove. Underneath it all—available steel-belted radials for cornering and FE2 rallye suspension to keep lean and sway in their place. Your place? Behind the wheel.

Can we build one for you?

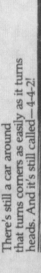

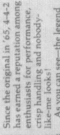

Special gauge cluster available

Olds 4-4-2 (above left). 1. Bucket seats, short-throw 5-speed overdrive manual shifter, available. 2. 4-4-2 has earned its stripes!

Oldsmobile again topped the million car mark this model year with 1,015,805 sales. The big divisional marketing move in 1978 came with the introduction of the 5.7 litre diesel engine on selected larger Oldsmobiles.

Once again, a completely restyled, and thoroughly downsized, Cutlass group was found on showroom floors. The W-29, or 4-4-2, package, again included a special grille, side stripes, rear and side numerals and the old stand-by, heavy-duty suspension. The new styling package blended well with the W-29 option. The W-29 could be ordered on the Cutlass Salon for $260 or the Cutlass Salon Brougham for $110.

A mild comeback was scored for the 4-4-2 in factory literature in 1978. A two-page spread was given the W-29 option (see pages 138-139).* One page was a later version of an American Grafitti street scene, while the second page examined the components of the 4-4-2 package with the aid of four photos.

*Front covers shown below.

CUTLASS 4·4·2

It draws a lot of attention.
Even standing still.

Precision instruments and sport wheel, available

With a reputation like 4-4-2's, you just might have to get used to stares at traffic lights and admiring looks at drive-ins.

For good reason. 4-4-2's street prowess is legend. But add the available 4-4-2 package to this 1978 Cutlass and you've got one impressive street car. A trim new size and 108-inch wheelbase make 4-4-2 agile. And

an improved power-to-weight ratio makes it feel more spirited than last year's 4-4-2!

FE2 rallye suspension, macho stripes and bold blacked-out grille—all included. And you can tailor 4-4-2 exactly to your liking. With new cast-aluminum sport wheels; 260 or 305 CID V8; 4-speed manual, 5-speed overdrive manual (except California) or

automatic shifter; dual sport mirrors—all available. Cutlass 4-4-2. A great feeling. The legend lives on!

Cutlass Salon 4-4-2 (far left). 1. Bucket seats, console, available. 2. Rallye suspension—with special spring rates, firm shock absorbers, plus front and rear stabilizer bars. 3. Take a test drive for fun. 4. Get an autographed copy!

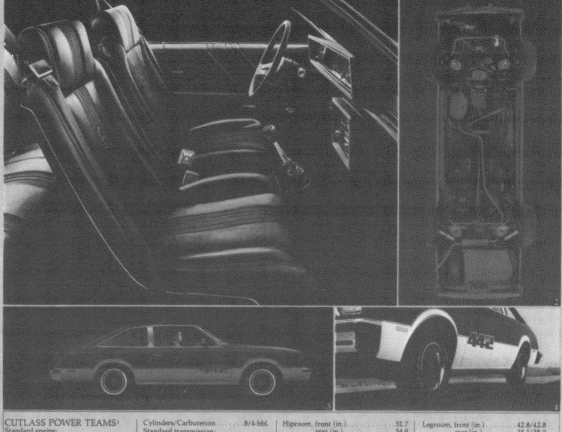

CUTLASS POWER TEAMS[1]						
Standard engine:		Cylinders/Carburetion	8/4-bbl.	Hiproom, front (in.)	51.7	Legroom, front (in.)	42.8/42.8

CUTLASS POWER TEAMS[1]

Standard engine:
CID/Type 231/V6
Cylinders/Carburetion ...... 6/2-bbl.
Available engines:
CID/Type 260/V8
Cylinders/Carburetion ...... 8/2-bbl.
CID/Type 305/V8
Cylinders/Carburetion ...... 8/2-bbl.
CID/Type 305/V8
Cylinders/Carburetion ...... 8/4-bbl.
CID/Type (Cruiser, high
altitude only) 350/V8

Cylinders/Carburetion .... 8/4-bbl.
Standard transmission:
Manual† .... 3-speed, all sync.
Available transmissions:
Automatic 3-speed
Manual*† .... 4-speed, all sync.
Overdrive manual**† 5-speed, all sync.
Fuel tank capacity (gal.) 17.5
DIMENSIONS (Supreme Coupe):
Overall length (in.) 200.1
Wheelbase (in.) 108.1
Headroom, front (in.) 37.9
rear (in.) 38.1

Hiproom, front (in.) 51.7
rear (in.) 54.9
Legroom, front (in.) 42.8
rear (in.) 36.4
Luggage capacity (cu. ft.) 16.1
Fuel tank capacity (gal.) 17.5
DIMENSIONS (Salon Coupe/Sedan):
Overall length (in.) 197.7/197.7
Wheelbase (in.) 108.1/108.1
Headroom, front (in.) 37.9/38.7
rear (in.) 38.2/37.7
Hiproom, front (in.) 51.7/52.2
rear (in.) 54.5/55.6

Legroom, front (in.) 42.8/42.8
rear (in.) 35.1/38.0
Luggage capacity
(cu. ft.) 16.4/16.1

[1]Check your Engine Supplement Sheet for specific details—standard and available equipment may differ in California and high-altitude areas.
*Available with 305 V8/2-bbl.
**Available with 260 V8 (all models), 231 V6 (Coupes with bucket seats only).
†Automatic only in California.
NOTE: Cutlass models will accommodate chains with standard tires only.

See EPA mileage estimates in the accompanying engine supplement sheet. Additional copies may be obtained from your Oldsmobile dealer.

17

Sparked by continued good sales of the diesel models, which by now included selected Cutlass models, Olds retained third place with a model run of 1,068,155. The best news in 1979, however, was that there was again a Hurst/Olds. Buyers eagerly purchased 2,500 of these Cutlass specialty cars.

Taking a page out of the not-too-distant past, Hurst tagged its H/O for 1979 a W-30. It came only on the Calais and added a hefty $2,054 to the base price. Either a black or a white exterior paint scheme could be ordered with the familiar gold stripes. This year's Hurst/Olds, as usual, was quite well appointed both inside and out. It was powered by a gasoline fueled 350 cid V-8, aluminum sport wheels, sport mirrors, raised white letter tires, sport console with Hurst shifter, power brakes, power steering, handling package, contour reclining bucket seats and full instrumentation. A total of 536 of the H/Os built in 1979 came with the T-top option.

Again, the 4-4-2 appearance and handling option—W-29—could be purchased. This year it cost $122 on either the Salon or the Salon Brougham coupe. Standard engine on all Cutlasses was the 231 cid V-6, so there are probably at least a few six cylinder 4-4-2s roaming the highways.

In the 1979 intermediate color catalogue, the 4-4-2 was again drastically cutback from the previous year's two-page spread. The 4-4-2 now held the bottom corner of a Cutlass Salon spread (see page 142).* A photo of the Hurst/Olds appears opposite.

*Front cover shown below.

Today, smart people are looking for space efficiency and fuel efficiency in the cars they buy. Make way for America's great new efficiency machine!

Designed from the inside out, Cutlass Salon is a car for today and for years to come.

Outside, Salon is trim, distinctive and handsome. Inside, it is impressively space efficient— with ample head- and legroom, front and rear.

The trunk, too, is space efficient, with an unobstructed floor and a compact spare that stands upright, out of your way.

But what really makes these dimensions exciting is that they have been achieved in a car that is nimble on the road, highly maneuverable in city traffic, and most importantly—fuel efficient!†

A smooth-firing, 3.8-litre V6 engine is standard. Or you can order a 4.3-litre or 5.0-litre V8 if you prefer.

But for the ultimate fuel efficiency in Salon, a new 4.3-litre diesel V8 is available—only from Oldsmobile!

We think you'll find Salon a tough value to beat at the price.

Come discover that great Cutlass Salon feeling! Take a test drive!

Cutlass Salon 4- and 2-door sedans (far left). 1. Bench seat in brushed woven, standard. 2. Special anti-corrosion measures include galvanized metals, plastisols, waxes and zinc-rich primers. 3. Bucket seats available. 4. The famous 4-4-2 with rallye suspension and its own special grille. The legend lives on!

*5-speed not available in California at start of production. Check your dealer for availability. †See EPA mileage estimates in accompanying Engine Supplement Sheet. 13

The official end of the line came for the 4-4-2 in 1980. Some sixteen years before, Oldsmobile put out the first 4-4-2 by pulling together some parts and components form the police pursuit package. By the late 1960s, and into the very early 1970s, the 4-4-2s and their heavily muscled cousins—the W-cars—ran off the showroom floor with the best iron Detroit could offer. It is curious that, in its last year, the 4-4-2 package once again used the W-30 designation. It is also curious that the 1980 4-4-2 was actually a lot closer to early Hurst/Olds offerings than it was to recent 4-4-2s.

Interestingly enough, the 4-4-2 package for this year was among the most complete and expensive ever offered. It did not, however, rival some of the earlier 4-4-2s in any aspect of performance level. The option listed for $1,255 and included a special grille, stripes, a specially modified 350 cid V-8 gasoline fueled engine, Rallye suspension, radial tires and a unique interior package.

The last official Hurst/Olds appeared in 1979 and the Hurst look-alike was issued as the final 4-4-2 in 1980. There were neither Hurst/Oldsmobiles nor 4-4-2's for 1981 or 1982. As we go to press with this volume, a Hurst/Olds has been officially announced for the 1983 model year. So, perhaps the legacy of the 4-4-2 and the Hurst/Olds may, indeed, not yet be dead...

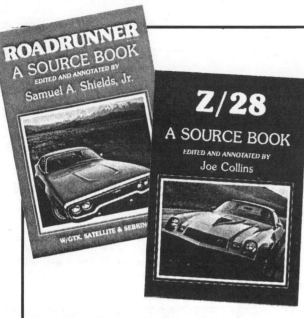